Killer Confession

Killer Confession
Double Murder Dialogue in Davis, California

By Lloyd Billingsley

A Centershot Book

Copyright © 2016 by Lloyd Billingsley

All rights reserved.

The persons and events in this book are factual. Any resemblance to fictional characters and imaginary events is entirely coincidental.

No part of this book may be reproduced or transmitted in any form or by any means, electronic or mechanical, including photocopying, recording or by any information storage and retrieval system, without written permission from the author, except for the inclusion of brief quotations in review.

Also by Lloyd Billingsley

Exceptional Depravity: Dan Who Likes Dark and Double Murder in Davis, California

Hollywood Party: Stalinist Adventures in the American Movie Industry

ISBN 978-0-9968581-3-7 (pbk.)

First edition 2016

Printed in the United States of America

1 2 3 4 5 6 7 8 9 10

For all who fought back.

Note on Names

The author will respect a court order protecting the identities of female minors here named Greta and Sally. The rest are unchanged from the official record, and all persons and events in this book are factual. Any resemblance to fictional characters and imaginary events is entirely coincidental.

Table of Contents

One: Without a Clue 1

Two: "I was kind of a weird kid, and a creepy kid." 3

Three: "The psychology behind it is fascinating." 23

Four: "I've got a whole plethora of hurts." 36

Five: "I'm a compassionate, affectionate person." 52

Six: "I'm just a scapegoat." 65

Seven: "Why would you fuck me over like this?" 73

Eight: "You're ruining my life." 83

Nine: "It felt great. Like it was pure happiness." 102

Ten: "I want to hurt people. I want to kill people." 115

Eleven: "She begged me to stop." 130

Twelve: Tortured Justice 140

Appendix: Autopsy Reports 142

Acknowledgements 158

"I'm a kid."
— Daniel Marsh

Chapter 1

Without a Clue

On April 14, 2013, police in Davis, California, received a call to check on an elderly couple at 4006 Cowell Boulevard in the south part of the city not far from Interstate 80, which runs right through town. Oliver "Chip" Northup, 87, an attorney and bluegrass musician with the Putah Creek Crawdads, had failed to show up for two gigs, and that was not like him. Chip was not answering his phone and neither was his wife Claudia Maupin, 76, an actress and pastoral associate.

Nobody answered the door at the couple's condominium where newspapers lay in the driveway. Police arrived after 9 p.m. and found the front door locked and the couple's car in the garage. Police also found a cut screen over an open window. Inside they saw a man covered in blood, stabbed multiple times, and disemboweled. The victim was Chip Northup, and police found that his wife Claudia Maupin had also been stabbed, slashed and eviscerated.

It was the first murder in several years in Davis, a low-crime college town just west of the state capital of Sacramento. The attack left police shaken, and officials at the Yolo County coroner's office had never seen such savagery. Davis police would charge that Oliver Northup and Claudia Maupin had been killed "in a way that manifested exceptional depravity" but they had no leads on the killer or killers.

Over the next two months, Davis detectives logged thousands of hours, chased down leads as far as Nevada, served 35 search warrants and generated 218 police reports. Davis police partnered with the Federal Bureau of Investigation, which tapped their National Center for Analysis of Violent Crime in Quantico, Virginia. By mid-June of

Killer Confession

2013 these marathon efforts rendered no suspects and police remained essentially without a clue. Then they got a telephone call from someone who claimed to know the perpetrator, and who revealed details that only someone at the crime scene could know.

That call led them to an address on East 8th Street, a stone's throw from Davis Cemetery, where murder victims Chip Northup and Claudia Maupin had been buried. Police picked up a slender youth, 16 years of age, and brought him to the Davis Police station on 5th Street. His name was Daniel Marsh, and as it turned out, he had a lot to say for himself.

Chapter 2

"I was kind of a weird kid, and a creepy kid."

"Okay Dan, Daniel, right?"

"Yeah."

"How are you doing? Ariel Pineda, detective."

"Nice to meet you."

"Hey. So, uh, you're in a police department, okay?" said Davis, California, police officer Eddie Ellsworth, who brought Dan into the room.

"So I have to read this stuff to you."

"Okay."

"You understand?"

"Yeah."

"You have the right to remain silent. Do you understand?"

"Yeah."

"Anything you say may be used against you in court. Do you understand?"

"Yep."

"You have the right to the presence of an attorney before and during any questioning. Do you understand?"

"Mm-hm."

"If you cannot afford an attorney one will be appointed for you free of charge before any questioning if you want. Do you understand?"

"Yeah."

"Okay," Ellsworth said. "Uh, do you want, basically, talk to Detective Pineda? He wants to talk to you and go over that stuff."

"All right."

"Hello Daniel," Pineda said, in a soft monotone.

"And I'll sit right here, okay," said Ellsworth. "I'll sit right here for you."

"Okay. Uh, I'm all right."

"You good?" said Pineda, "Can I get your name?"

"Dan Marsh."

"Is that your full name?"

"Well, Daniel William Marsh."

"All right," Pineda said. "How do you spell that? D-A-N. . ."

"I-E-L."

"D-A-N-E. . ."

"No, D-A-N-I-E-L, and William, just like normal spelling, and Marsh like M-A-R-S-H."

"Birth date?"

"May 14, 1997."

"What's a good phone number to reach you?"

He gave out the number, beginning with the 530 area code.

"Okay, a good address, too?"

"3306 Lillard Drive, L-I-L-L-A-R-D, Drive."

"Okay," said detective Pineda, "and student?"

"Yeah."

"At the high school? What year are you?"

"I'm going into my junior year."

"All right," said Pineda. "Okay. Well, Ellsworth went ahead and advised you of your rights per Miranda, and he's the one you had down here to question you. As you may know so we have an investigation going on in Davis in regards to some murders, and have some information indicating you may – know about it or you have some information as well. So that's why I'm here, to ask you about that, okay?"

"Okay," Marsh said.

"So, second question for you. Do you live alone?"

"No, I'm 16."

"I mean, do you have any sisters, brothers, you know, family?"

"Oh, it's just me, my mom. My sister lives with my dad."

"Okay. And you have a sister?"

"Yeah."

"Does she live with you too?"

"No, she lives with my dad."

"Okay," Pineda said. "So what is your dad's name?"

"Bill Marsh."

"And your sister's?"

"Sara Marsh."

"Is that with an 'H?'"

"No."

"Okay. And where do they live? Not – somewhere around Lillard?"

"Um, no, they live in Terracina, those low-ledged apartments by Nugget Fields."

"Oh, okay. That's off of Moore."

"Yeah."

"Okay, got it. All right," the detective said. "How is the school year for you?"

"Uh, stressful."

"Really?"

"Yeah," said Marsh. "Having issues early on in the year, then recovered from them, and then you know, more issues came along. I'm just glad it's over and I'm in summer right now, just kind of relax."

Pineda let a few beats pass before his next question.

"Was that during the school year, or was this later? Did it build up?"

"Um, it's like early on I had an issue with truancy and – which affected my grades, and then I recovered from that, got my grades up, and then like, uh, my issues didn't get worse but the environment I was in did, and the people I surrounded myself with didn't really help, and uh, it's just been a pretty stressful year."

"Okay. When you say environment, do you mean like home?"

"Home, school, friends."

"Quite a variety of things." Pineda's soft voice never varied in volume.

"Yeah, it's not fun."

"You have been able to deal with some of that stress?

"Uh, honestly, I smoke pot."

"Okay."

"Like, I don't do it for any other reason than to deal with my depression and my anxiety and all this shit that happens," Marsh said. "It's just kind of, you know, a little bit of relief temporarily. Like for a little bit I can just relax. I can just say 'Everything is all right now,' you know."

"Yeah. You been able to handle some of that stress with other people, anyone helping you out?"

"Um, well, yeah, uh, he picked me up from my friend's house today, Kevin, and uh, he's pretty much the only friend who's consistently been there. So he's helping me."

"How long have you known Kevin?"

"Uh, about a year."

"Does he go to school with you?"

"No, he graduated a year ago."

"Oh, okay, so you knew him from school."

"Yeah," Marsh said. "I met him senior year."

"Okay, so you've been hanging out with him quite a bit?"

"Yeah."

"How about, where is this? When you talk about depression, is it something where you are seeing someone professionally?"

"Yeah," Marsh said. "I was diagnosed a few years ago with severe clinical depression, and so since then I've been, you know, flying, kind of hopping around different psychiatrists and different medications."

"May I ask what, what you are taking for this?"

"Um, right now I'm taking Wellbutrin."

"What's that?"

"Wellbutrin," Marsh said, with crisp pronunciation. "It's just an antidepressant that works with your dopamine system."

"I see."

"And Zoloft, which is anti-depressant and anti-anxiety, and Abilify."

"How is that? Is your body, are you responding to that well?"

"It's helped, but not really a lot," Marsh said. "Like I've noticed a change but it's kind of plateaued to early on, I guess, would be a good way to put it. It like helped, but then it stopped and just like left me at that point of where it helped me."

"Okay," Pineda said. "So now describe how you're feeling at that point where, where you're left at, that a good place?"

"Um, well, it's better than before. Like, before I was, you know, I'd wake up and I didn't want to be alive and I didn't want to get out of bed. I didn't have any motivation to do anything, and now I get up, I like I shower, I get up, I take better care of myself, I eat better. Basically it pulled me out of rock bottom and put me on a little like, put me on my feet, I guess."

"Wow," said Pineda. "That sucks a lot."

"Yeah, it's . . ."

"When you talk about rock bottom, I mean, um, I've spoken to different teenagers and adults as well, rock bottom can mean many different things, and um, what is that to you?"

"Um, never feeling happy," Marsh said. "Just constantly feeling miserable, wanting to die, having such bad feelings of depression that actually it starts to physically ail you and you start to hurt, like your bones hurt, and it weighs you down. You just want to die so badly but you can't."

"Dan, again, I appreciate you telling us about that and I want to understand that. Is there some time? How far back are you talking about when this started?"

"Um, I was either 12 or 13 when I was diagnosed with it, but since I was like nine and my family kind of like broke."

"So nine years old? What do you mean broke? Your family, your parents split?"

"Yeah, like parents split," said Marsh, raising his volume a notch.

"Mom disappeared for a few months, left with dad, who was, well, he has a temper problem and you know, he just lost his wife so he's gonna be pissed off. So that wasn't really fun, and since then uh, every year it seems like you know, there's a new like bad thing to happen or a new crock of shit that he added in his pile."

Pineda listened intently.

"Where did you live, who were you living with when they split?"

"Um, I was living with my dad for the first few months, and then my mom came back from wherever the hell she was and got a duplex, and then I just kind of split my time. There was no like formal agenda, I guess. It was just, go where you feel like going."

"Mm-hm. So you were about nine years old. How did you deal with that at nine?"

"Uh, I don't know," Marsh said. "I kind of isolated myself. I didn't really have that many friends to begin with, but I just kind of pushed everyone away. I started doing home schooling and, and just kind of hung in my house, played video games, tried to deal with it. I also did martial arts for a while, so that was really helpful, actually. Did it for like four and a half or five years."

"Baciarini's, or?"

"Yeah. I was there when it was Pallen's."

"Pallen's, right, downtown?"

"Yeah."

Pineda seemed in no hurry.

"You have a sister?"

"Yeah."

"Is she older or younger?"

"She's older. She's 17."

"What was your sister's, your relationship with her at that time and that whole breakup?"

"Bad."

"Even way back then?"

"Yeah, she's actually, it's improved since back then," Marsh said.

"She was, she was a really bad attention-seeking habitual liar, a manipulator of my parents, and you know, when you are a little kid and you see that she's manipulating them and you try to tell them, they don't believe you 'cause you're just a kid. You don't know what's going on."

"Yeah."

"She's gotten better in that aspect since then," said Marsh.

"So you felt like she, you feel she's taken advantage in any way?" Pineda said. "Is that what you mean by manipulating situations?"

"Yeah, she would just kind of manipulate my parents to get them to do what she wanted them to do, and get them to believe things that weren't actually or hadn't happened. I don't know, she was like a little mini sociopath."

The detective betrayed no surprise at the teen's use of "sociopath."

"What direct effect did it have on you then?" said Pineda.

"Um, it made me feel really bad, 'cause it's like you know, I see the crap that's going on and I can't put a stop to it. I just have to sit back and just watch."

"Okay," Pineda said. "So you kind of feel responses. Did you feel like you could do something or not?"

"No. I tried but I couldn't do something, so I was just kind of like, just let the pieces fall where they may, you know."

"How was your relationship with your mom back then? Did she leave?"

"Yeah," said Marsh. "It wasn't good for. Well, it still isn't good."

"But you live with her?"

"Yeah."

"So what, what happened back then at nine? Or in that time when that breakup happened, your relationship with your mom?"

"Well," said Marsh, with no hesitation, "I was, I was pissed and I was hurt and I was confused and I didn't understand why she did what she did, or why she'd just up and leave like that, and why she's, you know, like in a child's eyes, it's like she destroyed the family, kind of, like why would you do that, why would you? I don't know, I was angry and confused about it, and I still don't really understand it."

"Okay," Pineda said. "So something you still haven't resolved within yourself, about like your mom did, or?"

"Yeah. I sort of get it, but it's still like, it was really selfish, honestly, 'cause she left with this, she left with a chick and I don't know what happened with that, but she was involved with my life for a few years. And I don't know, I just, my dad wasn't really, he never hit her. I mean, he could be, you know, an asshole sometimes."

"Okay," Pineda said.

"Just kind of blindsided me."

"Kind of happened and unfolded before you. Did you feel you could have a word in that or, or a say?"

"No, I tried but it didn't matter."

"How did you try?"

"Well, I talked to both my parents. I was like, 'why are you doing this?' Like 'this isn't necessary. Mom, you are being like, you're acting more childish than I am. Give you a problem, you don't want to run away from it.' But all she'd ever say to that was, 'No, I deserve to be happy. I deserve to be happy.' And that pissed me off because it's like 'Really? You care about your own happiness more than your children's?' That's, that's not right. I say, when you're a parent, kind of, you make it your duty to nurture your kids and take came of them and make sure that they're okay."

"Mm-hm, I see that," said the detective.

"Like they should come before you in a way, you know."

"Right. I get that."

"It's a commitment," said Daniel Marsh, 16. Pineda agreed.

"So you felt that didn't come from your mom, but that's what you believe?"

"Yeah."

"Should have happened, huh. Well, regarding your mom, similar still at this point? I mean, the years have gone by."

"Uh, now it's just weird," said Marsh.

"Like, she had a mental breakdown a long time ago, and since then she's never really been the same. And she got a bunch of neurological problems, and so they gave her a bunch of really heavy medications and like painkillers, and I think she's been taking advantage of that, because for years now, it's just like all the time, like medication, medication. It's heavy crap. It's like Dilaudid and anti-seizure drugs and I don't know. You can really see the effect it's had on her, like she went from having brown hair to now it's all white. Uh, she's only 47 and people will mistake her for being, like, a senior."

"Wow."

Marsh did not take the exclamation as a signal to slow down.

"Uh, mentally she's deteriorated a lot," the teen said. "Um, she's not really sharp anymore. Her personality's changed. I don't know. It's just kind of eating away at her and changed her into something she didn't use to be. So now it's just kind of weird, you know, you know, 'cause I don't really feel like she's my mom. It doesn't feel that way. It's just this chick that I live with."

"Wow," said Pineda. "That's pretty huge. And then you're living it. I, I'm just hearing what you are saying. You lived with your mom for how long?"

"Um, full on, with my mom for about a year and a half."

"For a year and a half, and this is what you're describing?"

"Yeah, it's just kind of . . ."

"Your whole life is?"

"Pretty much," Marsh said. "It's just kind of gone downhill. Before it was like, when she had the, she had fibromyalgia, well she still does, and trigeminal neuralgia, which is like, I don't know it, it affects your face specifically. It's like not just all nerves but they call it the suicide disease because the majority of people who get it kill themselves because of the pain. And so she had both of those at the same time. And so for a while me and my sister were kind of like the caretakers, nurses to her, in a way. So I guess that's, I don't know, she never really got better. Like she got to the point where she didn't need other people to take care of her, but she acts like she does."

"Okay. So you, you guys have been living, you and your mom have been living on Lillard here, 3306?"

"Yeah."

"For about a year and a half now?"

"No," Marsh said. "I think it's been like two, maybe three. Been there a while."

"Okay. And where did you live prior to that?"

"Um, well, we used to live in West Davis in a duplex, and then my dad had a house in west Davis, and then my mom moved to the Alhambra Apartments by Target, and then we got that place on Lillard, and then my dad moved to these apartments that, uh, I don't know what they're by."

"What was that?"

"Like deep south Davis," Marsh said. "Uh, my dad, I don't remember honestly. I, I didn't spend a lot of time over there. He like, he moved there and then . . ."

"Did you live with him?"

"For a little bit."

"Okay," Pineda said. "And was your sister living with him primarily?"

"No, it was, she was mainly living with my mom at the time."

"So your dad moved down south Davis. You said house, apartment?"

"Yeah, it was an apartment."

"Okay," Pineda said. "What, what was the address?"

The teen failed to respond with his usual speed.

"I, I don't remember," he said. "I know what it was like. I think they were neighbors of the people who got killed."

The teen's introduction of this theme, the subject of the interview, caused no change in the detective's demeanor or tone of voice.

"Okay," he said.

"Because I know like they were either next door or within like a few houses of there, actually, probably yeah. It is one of the main reasons that they moved from there to Terracina."

"Oh, tell me about that," Pineda said. "What do you mean?"

"Well, it freaked them out, you know."

"Okay."

"I mean, you wake up and you find like the people next to you turned dead. It was like, whoa, that could have been us, you know."

"Mm-hm."

"I, I guess it's just kind of, it's scary in a way. It's spooky. You're like, you want to just get out of there. I don't know, that's my perspective on that."

"So you stayed there a few times?"

"Yeah."

"With your dad? Okay. What's your relationship like with your dad?"

"Not good," Marsh said. "Um, the reason I've been living with my mom for a year and a half is because a year and a half ago he threw me out, and since then, up until recently I'd only had like a handful of interactions with him over the past year and a half, and then recently it's been getting more so, a little more often."

"When the, when you were nine back then when there was a breakup with your parents, what was your relationship like with your dad then?"

"Um, I guess it was all right," Marsh said. "I mean, he was really passive aggressive, and had a bad temper, and so I was never really comfortable, 'cause I feel like I'd say something and it would just like set him off and he'd get really pissed off. And so I don't know, I just kind of kept quiet um, around there."

"His temper, what was that like?"

"Uh, explosive," Marsh said. "He had, he never hit me or my sister, but he hit like the walls or he hit like inanimate objects. He'd yell and it's kind of that stereotypical just pissed off dad, only no physical abuse."

"He struck at other things and objects?"

"Yeah."

"Taking things out on the wall?"

"Yeah."

"What kind of things was he getting angry about?"

"Well," Marsh said, "at the time my sister was also living there, and I know she'd always make really big messes around the house, so she'd leave her stuff out all over the place or wouldn't clean her stuff up. She was, she didn't want to clean. She was a little brat, and he didn't really have the tolerance for that. He also has a lot of medical problems. Like he had a broken back that he had fixed and a broken neck which he got fixed. So he's also, and was also on heavy painkillers."

"Yeah."

"It's kind of, I don't know, it was weird," Marsh said. "And he'd be mellow and he'd just get really just pissed off, and then he'd be mellow again."

"How did you deal with that, personally?"

"Um, well, I mean around then was actually when I started doing the martial arts, and I just kind of, again, isolated myself and spent a lot of time in my room, just you know, if it's a problem, then I don't, I don't need that, you know. I don't need that kind of crap. I'm nine."

"How about with friends?" said Pineda. "It sounds like you've been isolating yourself in some way and the way you even tell me about your family. What about in regards to the social circles? Your family friends?"

"Well, I never really had that many friends," Marsh said. "I was like, uh, I was that loner kid, that you know, there's always that one outcast, like."

"Mm-hm."

"I was that one," Marsh said. "And so I've always had only a handful of friends, and lately because of the crap that's been happening, I've got like two or three left."

"Okay. Some of the crap you were telling me earlier, about your family?"

"Yeah."

"Okay, so two to three friends?"

"Yeah."

"Okay," said the detective. "You, you refer to yourself as a loner."

"Yeah."

"What does that, what does that mean to you?"

"Um, well, the other kids, you know, they pick on me and make fun of me and so I'd just, I'd sit in the corner basically. I just, I wouldn't talk to anybody. I'd just do my work and wait until I could go home."

"What were you getting, what are you getting picked on for?"

"Well, at the time," Marsh said. "I was actually kind of chubby and so they gave me crap for that, and I've kind of a weird, dark sense of humor, and so looking back on it, I was kind of a weird kid, and a creepy kid, in a way, but I'm not sure exactly what it was. They just didn't like me."

"There's specific things that were done? Or that you responded to?"

"Well, I, I got in a few fights."

"Yeah. Is that on campus?"

"No," Marsh said. "It was off."

"How long ago was that?"

"That was back in like junior high," Marsh said. "The last fight I got in was like ninth grade. It was for a different thing altogether."

"Yeah."

"Yeah, since I've gotten to, well, actually this year is kind of the first year that no one gives me any shit at school, so I guess in that aspect, it's not bad."

"Yeah," said Pineda, who had barely moved. "What, what dark sense of humor are you into?"

"Uh, you know those kind of jokes people is like, aw, you shouldn't say that, that's screwed up or, or like I'll laugh at you know, past tragic events, if there's a joke to be made out of it. Like, I'm not exactly proud of my sense of humor, but what makes me laugh makes me laugh, you know."

"Sorry to interrupt," said officer Ellsworth. "Do you want to uh, the lieutenant sent you a message just right here, sorry about that."

"Oh."

"For later in the week."

Pineda acknowledged the message and turned back to his questions for Daniel Marsh.

"So, you told me about the south of Davis apartment."

"Yeah."

"Did you live there with your dad?"

"Um, for a little while."

"Okay," Pineda said. "And that was approximately?"

"Like, almost two years ago."

"Two years ago, okay. And your sister was there with you at the time?"

"Um, no, she lived with my mom."

"She lived with your mom? So you lived with your dad?"

"Yeah, that's where we just kind of switched."

"Okay, and you went with your mom," Pineda said. "And you, so you, you do know about the murders that we're investigating here."

"Well yeah, obviously, I mean, it's Davis," Marsh said. "When something like that happens here, it's like, holy crap. Everybody knows about it, hears about it."

"Tell me what you know about it."

"Uh, I think they were an elderly couple or something?" Marsh said. "I know that somebody broke in, and like stabbed these two people, but I don't really know anything else. Breaking and entering, uh?"

"Do you know which apartment they lived at?"

"Uh, not the actual one, no, but I know it was like near my dad's," Marsh said. "I don't know, we drove by it a couple of times and we saw the police tape and everything."

"When was the last time you were there?"

"In that area?"

"Yeah."

"Uh, like a week after it happened or something like that," said Marsh. "It was soon enough to where there was still the tape up and everything. There were, all the cop cars were there, and there was investigators and stuff, and we drove by on the way to Target, and I was like . . ."

"So you know which unit?"

"Well, I do now."

"Yeah," Pineda said. "And do you know who lived there?"

"No."

"Okay."

"I heard that they were an elderly couple, but I never knew 'em."

The detective let more time lapse before speaking.

"Is there any other information that you know about what happened?"

"I can't think of anything," Marsh said. "Uh, I just heard the news reports and people talking about it at school. Somebody broke into their house, stabbed them to death and left 'em and I don't know. Not really."

"The week of school everybody started talking about it?"

"Yeah, well, not everyone but you know, word got around and people talked about it."

"Okay," Pineda said. "Do you know the weekend before the students started talking about it, what we're talking about? You know which weekend we're talking about?"

"I don't remember."

Pineda let the words linger.

"Dan," the detective said. "Do you think on April, the weekend of April 13th and 14th, can you tell me where you were?"

"I should have been at my house with my mom. On the weekends I usually just stay there."

"What were you doing?"

"Probably playing video games or playing guitar," Marsh said. "Usually what I do on my weekends is either I have somebody over or I just hang out and play video games or play music."

"What were you doing at your house?"

"Um, playing video games, laying around, sleeping, playing guitar."

"What, what do you normally play? What kind of video games?"

"Skyrim," Marsh said.

"Skyrim?"

"Yeah."

"Okay."

"Fallout three, just kind of you know, RPG games, long story, roaming and stuff."

"Do you play against others online?"

"Sometimes."

"You said maybe Kevin would know where you were and what you were doing that weekend?"

"Um, I doubt it," Marsh said. "But I, I'm pretty sure, like 99 percent sure I was at my mom's house but on the off chance that I wasn't, then I was at Kevin's house."

"You remember what you were doing that Friday night?"

"Um..."

"The twelfth?"

"Probably sleeping," Marsh said. "I mean, got off school, it's a Friday, so he has work. Usually what I do on Fridays is just stay home and go to bed."

"Okay," said Pineda. "What time do you usually crash?"

"Like 10 or 11," Marsh said. "I take sleeping pills to aid with that."

"And what do you do on Saturday?"

"Nothing, really, I just . . ."

"Do you remember that Saturday?" Pineda said. "Did you spend time with anyone?"

"Just my mom," said Marsh. "It's kind of difficult to remember the weekend when it was like two months ago."

"Understand" said Pineda. "Well, during this investigation we spoke to many people who also shared on that weekend, so we're going through the protocol and asking everyone what they did and where they were. So that Saturday evening, uh, the 13th, where were you? What were you doing? Do you remember?"

"I'm pretty sure I was just at my house, playing on my Xbox or playing my guitar."

"Xbox and guitar okay. Do you remember what games you were playing that night?"

"I think Black Ops 2."

"Black Ops 2?"

"Yeah, that's Call of Duty."

"Call of Duty," Pineda said. "Playing online with uh, any competitors or any strong competitors that challenge you?"

"No, I just online multi-player, just the general thing."

"What was that, online?"

"Just online multiplayer."

"Multi-player?"

"No, like competitions and anything."

"Yeah," Pineda said. "So is that, I don't play much video games, so you, you can tell me what you do but is that where you get random players from someplace else, or are you just playing alone?"

"Yeah. They um, they play into a lobby they call it."

"Mm-hm."

"And it's like depending on which type of thing you're going, they'll get a certain amount of players, and they try and get them that they are like people from your area so if they connect better and you just play with random people."

"Do you remember talking with anyone, chatting with anyone?"

"No, I don't usually."

"Don't remember being at Kevin's place or somewhere else?"

"No," Marsh said. "I'm pretty sure I was home."

"How long did you play video games that night?"

"A few hours."

"And then what'd you do?"

"Um, probably either played guitar, or depending on the time, went to bed."

"What do you remember next?" the detective said.

"Um, I think on Sunday it was when me, Kevin and Josh, and Alvaro went to Guitar Center, I think. It was either that weekend or the next weekend."

"Okay."

"Uh, I know that was a lazy weekend, and I didn't really do anything other than lie around or hang out with a couple of friends."

"Where was that at?"

"Where was what?"

"Where'd you guys hang out?"

"Uh, either Kevin's or maybe Alvaro's."

"Alvaro?"

"Yeah."

"What's uh, Alvaro's full name?"

"Alvaro Garibay."

"And you said Kevin's was uh, Green?"

"Yeah."

"Who was the other friend you may have been with?"

"Uh, Josh," Marsh said.

"Josh?"

"O'Guinn," Marsh said. "It's like O, apostrophy, G-U-I-N-N."

"You're saying, you think that was Sunday?"

"Yeah, I think so."

"So you hung out together at possibly Garibay's place?"

"Possibly, yeah."

"What'd you guys talk about?"

"I don't remember," Marsh said. "Like, I don't know, it was, like what's today? I don't know. It was either two months ago or over two months ago, so I don't, I don't remember specific conversations, 'cause I know we didn't talk about anything important."

"Okay," said Pineda. "Well, you remember when we first brought you in here and I asked you questions and regarding information that we had that led you to believe that you have information or you know things about the murder investigation that we're doing. And we're doing a thorough job in talking to everyone, that's connected to and, I just wanted to make sure you're telling me what is gone on and what happened this weekend is the truth. So you know we're going to do our investigation, and we're continuing to do that even as we speak here in regards to what happened that weekend. And that weekend, Friday night, Saturday night to Sunday, and you return back to school Monday, this is what you're saying you did and who you were with, and they would say the same thing?"

"Well, I honestly, I don't remember if it was that weekend or the next weekend, that I hung out with them and went to Guitar Center," Marsh said. "But I'm, if it was that weekend, then that's what I did. If it wasn't, then I did the same thing I did on Saturday and just laid around. I didn't really, I don't do that much other than hang around with people and play my music, play games."

"Yeah," Pineda said. "Well, I'm also trying to clear up some things, maybe some rumors, and maybe some information in regards to you and the murder investigation we're doing on the murder that happened on Cowell. Is there anything you can tell me?"

"I haven't heard any of these rumors that you, like, I haven't heard anything about it," Marsh said. "I haven't heard anybody say anything about me in regards to it. Like honestly, I haven't heard anything about me in regards to that. I don't know why it would be there, why people would, anyone would spread a rumor."

During the pause, detective Pineda maintained eye contact with the teen.

"What if it becomes more than a rumor?" Pineda said. "What if we have more information that you may have something to do with it?"

"But I don't."

"How can you prove to me that you, you don't?"

"Well, I'm pretty sure if you ask my mom, she'll say I was there. Um, I don't know. How would anybody else prove that? I mean, I know if, if you're looking for an alibi that that would be it, but I had nothing to do with it. I was, it was just a lazy weekend."

"So what did you guys do at Guitar Center?"

"Tested out amps," Marsh said. "I played a few guitars in the basements, just what we usually do. They've got, I don't have like a good amp. I've got this crappy little 15 Watt, and as, and as my friends don't have good equipment, and so it's fun to go there and mess with the big amps that have like tubes and $2,000 guitars and everything."

"What were the other guys doing?"

"Same thing. Me and Alvaro both play the guitar, and so we were both messing around with that, and Josh plays bass."

"What'd you guys buy?"

"I don't know if we bought anything," Marsh said. "I think Alvaro bought strings."

"How'd you guys get around?"

"Well, Kevin's 19. He has a car and a truck."

"So you're saying he drove you guys?"

"Yeah, when he went."

Pineda remained still as a statue.

"So, Daniel," he said after another long pause. "With regards to the two murders at Cowell that you told me you knew about."

"Yeah, I heard about it."

"What other information, or what else can you tell me about what happened to them?"

"All I really know is somebody broke in and, and I think I'm, it was like they were stabbed and maybe beaten to death. I don't know if that was put in. Yeah, it was, I really don't know anything else other than that. Somebody broke in and. . ."

"What was that now?" Pineda said. "That they were stabbed and what?"

"Possibly beaten to death," Marsh said. "I think that was in one of the news reports."

"Yeah. What else?"

"That's it," Marsh said. "Um, I don't, I didn't do like research on it. I don't know much about it, just someone broke in and did something really horrible to those people."

"Such as?"

"Well, he killed them."

"Who did?"

It was a question of some pertinence. But before Marsh could answer, officer Ellsworth excused himself to take a phone call.

"I don't know if it was a he, I don't if it was a she," Marsh said. "I don't know if it was a group of people. I, but whoever did it did something horrible to those people who I assume didn't deserve it. I don't know what else you want me to say. Really I don't know anything other than that. Just somebody broke in and from what I've heard, just killed two innocent people. I don't know why, I don't know who. I don't really have anything to do with them. Sorry if I'm like, not much help with this or anything. I just . . ."

"Like boots?"

"What?"

"Like boots?'

"Do I like boots?"

"Yeah."

"Um, I guess," Marsh said. "I, I don't really have a preference of shoes. I have boots. I have Converse."

"Has that other issue been resolved in school?"

"Which issue?"

"Yesterday, there's a case I the school I think I read on a call before, you were in possession of a knife."

"Oh, yeah," Marsh said. "That's, um, it's being resolved. Actually, today we were supposed to have a meeting that would kind of decide what the course of action would be, but it's been moved on to either Tuesday or Thursday, so it's being resolved."

"Did you have a knife on you?"

"Um. Yeah, I did."

"What kind of knife was that?"

"Um, Benchmade."

"Folding knife?"

"Yeah."

"Do you have any other knives you keep at home?"

"No," Marsh said. "I own, no, just uh, like kitchen cutlery, you know. I don't own any like knives or weapons of my own."

"You got any other knives?"

"I mean, they're not mine, no."

"Whose knives are they?"

"My mom's," Marsh said. "I mean, we have a kitchen, so we have like that stereotypical kitchen knife set."

"What other knives do you guys have in the house?"

"I know she has a pocket knife," Marsh said. "Uh, I know we have a few swords, but that's just 'cause you know, I went to Japan Town, or I went to the Renaissance Fair. Actually one of them is also from an anime convention."

"Where are those at?"

"Where are they? Um, in my garage."

"Does your mom keep any knives for herself?"

"Um, all I know is that she has the pocket knife."

"How about yourself?" Pineda said, "Any more?"

"No, I only had that one."

The voice of officer Eddie Ellsworth interrupted the session.

"Okay. They're in here."

Chapter 3

"The psychology behind it is fascinating."

"Hey Ariel," said the man who had entered. "How are you doing? Good to see you." He turned to Marsh.

"Hi."

"Hi."

"You must be Daniel?"

"Yeah."

"I'm Chris Campion."

"Nice to meet you."

"Nice to meet you," Campion said. "I'm from the FBI. Work around here, and I do kind of some of the criminal profiling stuff, and been working with Ariel on this case since it happened. So sorry I'm a little late."

"It's all right," Pineda said.

"You guys been talking. Eddie told me you guys have been talking a little bit."

"Yeah."

"Sounds like this young man has quite a history," said Campion, who could pass for a high-school teacher. "Kind of a family train wreck, if I can be so bold to say that."

"Yeah, pretty much," Marsh said.

"So what I hear, I mean, dad and mom split when you were pretty young?"

"Yeah."

"Wow, and then mom basically left, abandoned you, or your family?"

"Yeah, for like three or four months, and she just kind of ran away, turned up again."

"And any explanation, or any apologies?" Campion said.

"No. She just kind of acted like it didn't happen. She just kind of got a duplex and move on."

"Wanted to just pretend it didn't happen."

"Pretty much," Marsh said. "She doesn't like to deal with problems."

"Oblivious to the effect it had on you?"

"Basically."

"And what, what was the effect that it had on you? I mean, that's got to be devastating."

"Uh, yeah, it sucks. It sucked. It made me, I'm pretty sure that's around the time that all this depression stuff probably got kicked off."

"Uh-huh."

"It made me feel shitty. It's like it's my family and it, it just fell apart right in front of me."

"Disintegrated and there's nothing you as a . . . how old were you?"

"Nine."

"A nine-year-old can do about that."

"Yeah."

The FBI man proceeded at a brisk pace.

"What was your dad's reaction?"

"Uh, he was shocked and pissed off."

"Wow," Campion said. "I would imagine. I mean, that's gotta. . ."

"Well, yeah, I mean. . ."

"Create a lot of rage in a man. I mean, his wife just takes off. And then Eddie just said something real briefly that she came back with another woman or something?"

"Mm-hm, oh, yeah. She, um, it was actually my kindergarten teacher."

"Wow."

"Yeah."

"So your kindergarten teacher shows up back in your life."

"Yep."

"When you're nine," Ellsworth said. "So you're what, fourth grade by then maybe?"

"That's the woman that my mom was having an affair with and left with."

"Wow," said Campion.

"Yeah."

"Well, that's got to be devastating, shocking."

"Yeah, it, it blindsided me."

"Well, yeah, as a nine-year-old," Campion said. "I mean, do you really even comprehend the fact that there's the, you know, a romantic relationship between your mom and this woman?"

"No, I didn't really understand it."

"Wow. So that probably added to your dad's anger and whole sense of insecurity?"

"Oh, yeah. He talked a lot of crap about that woman."

"Wow," Campion said. "Wow, so unstable doesn't begin to even address it. What the, I'm just guessing, tell me what the household is like, I mean. I mean, do they get back together at some point then, or was it one of those, it kind of went on and then off and then on and then off?"

"No, it was just off."

"Off, okay. Did you ever felt like anybody blamed you, Daniel?"

"No. If anyone, I felt like some of the blame was put on my sister, but rightfully so."

"Rightfully so?"

"Yeah."

"How so?" said Campion. "What did she do to cause this?"

"Uh, she was a habitual liar and she manipulated my parents, like tell one of them did something that they didn't to get a certain thing from the other, to get like a reaction. Uh, I feel like she just did it for the attention, but it was still screwed up."

"Kind of like using each other?"

"Yeah."

"Using one to get to the other?"

"Yeah."

"Now, did she do that – is she older than you or younger than you?"

"Yeah, she's older than me."

"Did she do that before your parents split up?"

"Yeah."

"Or was that kind of her reaction?" Campion said. "So this was all before?"

"Yeah and after."

"And after. And still today?"

"Uh, to a lesser extent."

"Okay."

"Not nearly as bad as it was."

"Okay. Wow. That is a tumultuous place to be as a nine-year-old. So where did you go? What did you do with that? As a nine-year-old, where did you seek refuge?"

"You mean, where did I live or where did I?" Marsh said. "What did I do to cope with it?"

"Well, both. I mean, more the coping. How did you survive it?"

"Well, around that time I started martial arts, and that really helped, you know. It helped me get, you know, blow off some steam, get some positive endorphins going, make me feel good and keep my mind off everything. It actually taught me a lot of like self-discipline and self-control and it, it really helped a lot."

"And how long did you do that then?"

"Like four and a half years."

"Okay," said Campion. "So nine to ten till when?"

"Probably till I was like, I think I stopped when I was 14."

"And how old are you now?"

"Sixteen."

"Sixteen," Campion said. "So a year or two ago you stopped?"

"Yeah, I stopped when I got my black belt?"

"You got your belt, black belt?"

"Yeah."

"In which discipline was it?"

"It was first degree Philippine martial arts."

"Oh, okay. And there's a place in Davis that does that?"

"Yeah, uh, it used to be called Pallen's, but now it's Baciarini's that big studio. It's by the Dairy Queen and the railroad tracks."

"All right," said Campion. "So you, did you spend a lot of time there, or would you practice at home?"

"Um, yeah, I spent a lot of time there, but since I stopped I don't."

"Right. Did you have any friends from there, any people that you know, you worked out with or people that you got to be close with there?"

"Not really friends," Marsh said. "I was um, the closest thing to friends were like the instructors. They had like, I mean, like I guess you could call it Sensei or the big cheese in the studio."

"Mm-hm. Yeah."

"And then he had like I don't know what you call 'em, other instructor that were like second degree black belts. Uh, they were nice to me."

"They were nice to you. So they were, they were good?"

"Yeah."

"I mean, that's, you know what that means, right. That comfort, that area where you can get away from your problems for a bit."

"Yeah."

Campion maintained an even pace.

"What other things," he said, "would you be able to do to get away from all those problems?"

"Played a lot of video games."

"Okay, like most kids your age, yeah."

"Yeah."

"And what are your favorite ones?"

"Uh, I think I'd go with classics and be like Ratchet and Clank, uh, Legend of Zelda."

"Retch and Clank?"

"Uh, Ratchet."

"Ratchet, okay."

"Yeah, um. Super Smash Brothers."

"Okay. What was the second one you said?"

"Legend of Zelda."

"And what's that one about?"

"Uh, it's like uh, it's weird. You're in like this fictional world, and you're like people but you have pointy ears but you're not called elves, and you just go around on an adventure, because some evil presence is like destroying the world and you have to stop it."

"Wow."

"You know, it's like this big adventure game," Marsh said.

"There's several to the series, and it's pretty fun, enthralling."

The FBI man was intrigued.

"So you go around the world, and like what, what kind of things do you do? What are your tasks to do?"

"Um, basically it's that, beat the bad guys and the one I played, like your sister got kidnapped and so the main thing was like to find her."

"Okay."

"And save your sister."

"Which maybe you didn't want to try that hard to save your own sister."

"Kind of ironic."

"So what kind of things would you have to do to save her? What kind of challenges would you have?"

"Uh, you travel around, like solve puzzles, fight monsters."

"Like puzzles," Campion said. "What kind of puzzles?"

"Uh, like there's, I think the one I remember best is like there's a bunch of blocks and they each have different markings on it, you have to move them around to make like a certain shape to illustrate it on like, it's like on the side of the wall but it's hidden. That game made you really think, and like try and look around, use your surroundings to try and figure out what you're supposed to do."

"Okay. Interesting. So kind of just you'd have to be there. You're the first person I assume right, or are you looking at them from top?"

"I'm third person."

"Third person, okay. Um, and then you would send yourself, you sent other people to go do things?"

"Um, you'd do it."

"You'd do it," Campion said.

"You're, you're like a kid teenager age, so you're kind of on your own, in this big adventure as well. It's pretty cool."

"Interesting. Ariel, I hate to do this to you, but could you, could I grab, get a glass of water? Did you, do you want something, Daniel?"

"No."

"Refill? Do you need anything else, bathroom, phone call, do you have to do anything this afternoon?"

"No."

"Are you good for talking here for a little while?"

"Yeah, I can talk."

"Okay," Campion said. "Anytime you want to do any of those things, let me know, all right?"

"Okay."

"Sorry, I got this stuff in my, pollen in my throat or something. So, well, the refuge is, is huge. I mean, doing the kind of work that I do, there is, I see lots of people who have had lives that are just devastated, devastated by all sorts of things, and the refuge is the key. And we all do that, I mean from combat veterans in Afghanistan and Iraq who come back and they have these nightmares and they're haunted."

"PTSD and stuff?"

"PTSD, right," Campion said. "We see those and we see then do just some horrible things because they just want the, the pain to stop. They want the, they need the refuge. They need someplace to go where they can feel something besides what they are feeling. Does that make sense to you?"

"Yeah, it's a way to escape," Marsh said. "To get some temporary relief."

"Right. Temporary relief from the hell that they're living in."

"Yeah."

"Does that sound kind of familiar to you?"

"Yeah."

"Eddie said something about feeling suicidal and depressed at various times in your life. I guess he works with you at the school sometime?"

"Yeah."

"Or has in the past?"

"Off and on, from Youth Academy."

"From the Youth Academy, right. Oh, here at the Police Department, they have one of those?"

"Yeah."

"Those youth academy programs."

"I did that," Marsh said. "It was pretty cool, actually. Yeah, learned a lot."

"Yeah?"

"Yeah."

"What's your thought about cops here in Davis?"

"Um, well, about half of them are cool people, and the other half are just kind of dicks."

"Yeah?"

"I feel all they do is just pick on people, and like pick on teenagers. Like, they wait by the junior high because they know kids don't have helmets, so they can ticket them."

"Oh really?"

"It's like, you don't have something better to be doing," Marsh said. "You're a cop, come on."

"Yeah," Campion said. "So about half and half, huh?"

"Pretty much."

"All right. I've got to know Ariel a little bit, and I think he is, uh, no dick. And I just met Eddie for the first time today, so don't know him at all. He seems like an okay guy."

"Yeah," Marsh said. "I think he's a pretty cool guy."

"Or does he have to write tickets and all that kind of stuff at the high school?"

"No, I haven't seen him do that," Marsh said. "He just, I don't know, there are people who do their job as a cop just 'cause they want to feel powerful."

"Yeah."

"And then there are people who genuinely care about other people and just want to help. You know, they want to help with society and the community, and I think that he's one of those."

"Daniel, that is very well put," Campion said. "That was very well put."

Marsh seemed momentarily impressed with himself.

"People call you Daniel or Dan? What do you usually go by?"

"Uh, usually Dan."

"Dan, all right," Campion said. "That is wise beyond your years, because, and I would put it, probably in, in law enforcement just Davis Police Department, but we travel a fair amount in the FBI and we see a lot of different law enforcement people around the state, around the country. I go overseas sometimes and work with the police over there. And it's about half and half, and half of the people are just, it's kind of a power thing."

"Yeah."

"You know, it's kind of you know, 'I'm, I'm going to tell you what to do.'"

"Exactly."

"And the other half, it's a helping thing, and it's funny before I even knew I wanted to go into law enforcement, when I was a really young, my girlfriend at the time convinced me to go and see a psychic, or a palm reader she was, actually. And so she kind of read my palm and did the whole thing. I don't know if you believe in any of that stuff at all."

"Not really," Marsh said.

"I was pretty skeptical, to say the least," Campion said. "When this was happening I was a little older, maybe 18, 19 years old. And she looked at my hands, and I don't know what lines she's looking at or whatever, and she says 'You're going to be a healer. That's what you're gonna do with your life.' And my dad was a doctor, and I said, 'There's no frigging way I want to be a doctor. I, you know, I want to do something outside, I want to do something where I meet a lot of people, not everybody who's sick, you know, all that kind of stuff.' And years later when I started doing this, and especially this kind of work, where I'm dealing with violent crimes and, and profiling and stuff like that, at one point, 'cause she said 'I see you standing in front of a group of people and I can't tell what language they're speaking. It's not Spanish, it's not German and, but they look kind of German, and you're standing in from of this group of speaking people and speaking about healing.' And so a few years ago I was in Brazil and I'm up in front of a group teaching a bunch of law enforcement people about some stuff that we do. And they're, they're talking in Portuguese, but they look like German, and you know, kind of Aryan-type folks."

"Mm-hm."

"And I'm, you know 'Boys from Brazil' and all that. You, it might be before your time."

"Yeah," Marsh said. "I know what you are talking about."

"You know what I'm talking about, and I'm like, 'holy smokes. Could it be that I really did see something?' Because I was talking about healing and law enforcement and, and not necessarily just the victims but the people who do these horrendous things, what the public perceives as horrendous things."

"Yeah."

"And understanding what's going on and why and everything is a healing. And then I'm like, 'holy smokes there is something to that.'

I don't know maybe, but I think it was about 50/50 throughout law enforcement. Maybe 70/30. So that's where I come from. That's the point of view where I come from. That's more my interest in this, is to try to see through, cause there's a lot of people who, who just, you know, whoever would do a thing like this, an animal and, and you know, needs to be put away for whatever."

"Mm-hm," said Marsh. "I look at it like, people do horrible things, but that doesn't necessarily make them horrible people."

"Yeah," Campion said. "Again, very perceptive."

Campion requested more water.

"So I was getting this, I think I got too much pollen or something in me today."

"I thought allergies were supposed to be over for the summer," said Marsh, who also got a water refill from Pineda.

"Yeah, I traveled a lot. Like I said, I was down in San Francisco last week, I was up in Lake Tahoe this week, and now I'm here today, so I don't know where I picked, where I pick up stuff."

Campion paused briefly.

"So, um, where are we?"

"You were talking about how, first you were talking about healing and then you were talking about how society perceives the people who do horrible things."

"Yeah, and, and I agree with you," Campion said. "They're not horrible people. I think a lot of them get to a point where they do it because it's all they can do. That's all they can do. They don't like have a choice. It's to that point where, for whatever reason, there's a lot of different ways, a lot of different pathways that we get to that point, of where we have this one thing that is like a compulsion. You know what that is?"

"Yeah."

"Okay."

"Something second nature, can't really help it."

"Yeah, second nature for whatever reason. I mean, whatever the reason. I mean, some people, you know, wash their hands all the time."

"Yeah."

"Like the classic obsessive compulsive person. Um, some people you know, view pornography all the time, and some people you know, have something in their mind that says, that the only thing I can be sexually attracted to is young children. Yeah, there is a little bit of the yuck factor. But for me, it's like, okay, so what made that person so fascinated with, you know, young children?"

"Yeah," Marsh said. "The psychology behind it is fascinating."

"Yeah."

"Because there's so many like millions of different aspects that could have led them to the way they are now."

"Yeah, exactly, and it's never-ending," Campion said. "And you know, you could read about it in a textbook, you could read about it in professional articles, you can do that, and we all do that. But until you're sitting and talking to someone and they are saying, okay, here's why I'm, I'm sexually attracted to children and nothing else, no one else. I mean, you could have whoever the most beautiful woman or man in the world is, you know, standing right in front of them, but they would prefer you know, an eight-year-old child to Brad Pitt or Angelina Jolie, you know. That's just where their mind has gone in terms of the wiring, it's the biology and the chemistry and the physiology of it, that puts them there."

Marsh appeared to be listening intently. Campion continued.

"And it's really interesting, the psychology is that, you know, and is, there's all of these theories but when you talk to a guy like that, and, and sometimes they're very open and honest, and, and it's really refreshing and I think it actually helps them in the long run, because it makes people understand that they maybe didn't choose to be in this place. They didn't choose to wanting to you know, go to public pools so they can get sexually arouse by eight-year-old girls and go masturbate in bathrooms. That's not what they planned for their lives, right? But when did you get there? How did you get there? And I ask them, you know, and they're sometimes very honest. And they say, 'Chris, it's just, I, I can't not do it. I can't not have it. It's what I think about all the time.'"

"Hm," Marsh said. "Sounds like it might be a form of OCD."

"It's an obsession for sure," Campion said, "and it's a compulsion because they can't not do it. So it's like an obsession. It's a compulsion. They can't not do it, but the point is that something happened. And for a lot of these guys, it's when they were that age, that they were molested, or maybe they were just a little bit older and they were molested by someone, sometimes a close family member. You know, father, brother, uncle, boy scout leader maybe, someone in their community, priest, um you know, somebody they trusted. And you know what they say they're looking for, Daniel? They're looking for something that, it just choked me the first time one of them said to me, 'do you have any idea?' They're, they're looking for innocence."

"Really?"

"They're looking for something they lost."

"Hm."

"They lost that innocence, right along that time, and they want to be around that innocence again, that time where you didn't have people messing with you and, and doing things to you that you don't want them to do."

"Like before the like main tragedy that completely changed their psyche happened, right?"

"Yeah, yeah," Campion said. "So that's what I try to understand and what we try to work on, healing and talking about it. And like I was saying, we're talking about different reasons people are in law enforcement, Ariel, and cops who want to help and want to heal, versus cops who just want to put people in jail and think that they're, they're dirtbags or whatever."

"Mm-hm," said Ariel Pineda.

"So, anyway," Campion continued. "It's pretty interesting work, and that's what we do and what I do. Like I was telling Dan that time, you know, you and I have only worked together for a couple of months, but I feel like you're, you're one of the guys who does want to help and heal. Just from what I've seen with you."

Marsh jumped back in with no prompting from either man.

"What else is interesting about the psychology, is every, from what I researched, I think it's called what matter that goes in your brain, and every decision or choice you make or action or impulse you get into, it changes the pathways in your brain."

"Yeah," said Campion.

"Literally everything you do, just, it changes it so your brain is constantly changing, rewiring. I guess at some point something can just go wrong."

"Yeah," Campion said. "Where did you read about that? Or where did you hear about that?"

"I actually heard it from my principal."

"Okay. And did he say, how did it come up in the conversation?"

"Well, actually we were talking about House and medical stuff like that."

"About a house, oh House? The TV show?"

Marsh nodded.

"Oh, okay, and so what was the connection there?"

"Oh, we were talking about like his personality and wondering like, you know, 'Why is he the way he is?' And she was like, 'Oh, hey, have you heard about this study?'"

"Oh, so your principal is a she. So she brings this up."

"Yeah."

"About the TV show. Okay, interesting."

"Seemed kind of a non sequitur at the time," Marsh said. "But I was interested."

"Yeah. I think it's very true, and you know think about in, DNA and the way that our cells are formed and you know, the cells going together to make tissue and bone and all that kid of stuff and then neuroneurons in your brain and constantly being regenerated and all of that. It's just fascinating to me. You know, what are the odds it's going to work exactly like its supposed to all the time?"

"Yeah."

"None," said Campion. "I mean, you know, it doesn't just happen. Nothing's perfect in this world. Nothing's perfect at all. So anyway, that's just a little bit about me and why I'm here and trying to help you."

Marsh did not respond. Campion turned to detective Pineda.

"What, Ariel, how far have you gotten in talking with Daniel about what he's here for?"

"Um, I just asked him what he knew," the detective said. "What he knows about the, murders in south Davis and trying, opening that up."

"Okay."

"Asking him where he may have been, that particular weekend, who he was with. Is that about right Daniel?"

As the hitherto talkative Marsh hesitated, Campion pressed the point.

Chapter 4

"I've got a whole plethora of hurts."

"What do you know, Dan?"

"Um, about that or about where I was?"

"About the murders," Campion said.

"Oh," Marsh said. "I just know that somebody broke into this old couple's house and stabbed them, killed them."

"Okay. And I understand it's fairly near to some place that you know fairly well?"

"Yeah, it was near my dad's house."

"Okay. And he then left?"

"Yeah."

"Left after that?"

"I'm not sure," Marsh said. "I think it had something to do with that spooked him, and then at the same time his landlady died, and so the kids were trying to sell the apartment that he was in."

"Okay."

"And so it was just kind of like an extra reason like, 'all right, let's just get out of here.'"

"Okay, So that must have been, what, what's your dad's name?"

"Bill."

"Bill," said Campion. "So when we were there, remember, a couple of days later, not the first time we went around and talked to everybody but the second time when we all went down there, there was that house. Is, is it two down or three down from the place where the people lived that were killed?"

"I'm not exactly sure," Marsh said. "It, I know if you're looking for my dad, he's kind of an old dude with either a weird mustache or a beard."

"Yeah."

"Kind of long hair."

"So one of the police officers talked to him right after," Campion said. "And then he, by the time we came back like three or four days later he had moved out. Does that sound about right, like the right time frame?"

"Something like that."

"Well, what do you remember?" said Campion. "I shouldn't ask it that way. What do you remember about how long after the cops left that he left? Excuse me."

"I think it was either a week after or two weeks later."

"Okay."

"He didn't really waste any time," Marsh said. "You know when the landlord is pushing you, like you gotta get out of there and something like that happens right next to him. It's like, 'alright, let's try and find a place.'"

"Okay."

Marsh's phone rang.

"I'm sorry," he said. "I'll turn that off."

"Is that a text or a call?"

"Oh it was a call but I didn't recognize the number."

"All right," Campion continued. "So a week or two weeks after. That's about right. I think we were there like a week or ten days later."

"A little after that," Pineda said.

"That house had been vacant."

"You spoke with your dad," Pineda asked Marsh, "or sister that you talked to about and then moved in?"

"I talked to my sister about it."

"Oh, okay," Pineda said. "What did she tell you?"

"About them moving?"

"Yeah."

"Well she told me that you know their landlady died and her kids were trying to sell the place and that her and her boyfriend at the time and my dad were all freaked out because of what happened. You know the murders, and uh, actually my mom had been looking for a place to move to because we thought that we were going to have to move out of our house and we found those Terracina Apartments and apparently it was in their budget so they moved there."

"And your mom didn't end up moving there?" Campion said.

"No, we're still where we were."

"Okay. All right."

Campion's phone sounded, but he didn't recognize the number.

"So we're still looking, you were in the neighborhood and how often would you go to that house?"

"I wouldn't," Marsh said. "My dad, my dad threw me out like a year and a half ago. I haven't been back to that house since."

"Oh really? A year and a half prior?"

"Yeah."

"To now?"

"Yeah."

"Oh."

"I've only had like a handful of interactions with him since then and recently had a few."

"Okay," said Campion. "So I mean you would go over there to visit or you obviously knew where he was, right?"

"Yeah. I knew where he lived but I didn't really go over there."

"But not as part of regular custody?"

"Uh-huh."

"Back and forth?"

"No," Marsh said.

"Did you have a room there?"

"Um, yeah," Marsh said. "Well, I did but he made it into like office space."

"He made the office space in your room?"

"Yeah."

"And there was a room for your sister or was she pretty much moved on?"

"She had a room too."

"Okay. And who else lived there with your dad?"

"Uh, her boyfriend."

"Your sister's boyfriend?"

"Yeah."

"Okay. And what's his name?"

"Brian. All right," said Campion. "Hold on for a minute, will you write that down? Brian. So what's Brian's deal? Is he an okay guy or?"

"He's a great guy."

"Oh good."

"Yeah."

"You like him?"

"Yeah," Marsh said. "Uh, he lived with, before my sister move out and moved in with my dad, her and Brian lived with my mom and I. And me and Brian, we'd like, we'd actually hang out a lot. We'd talk, you know shoot the shit, and talk about what's going on in our lives and he's really a good guy. He's really polite, well mannered and cares about people. And he wanted to, he just wanted to help."

"Okay."

"Like yeah, he's a really good guy."

"And is he older than your sister? In school with you guys or is he older or?"

"He's 19, she was 17."

"Okay. Does your sister go to school?"

"Yeah."

"And does Brian, or is he gone? He's done now?"

"He's not, he's not done."

"And what does he do during the day?"

"He works in Dixon in the warehouse with his dad."

"Do you know his last name?"

"Harty," Marsh said. "Like H-A-R-T-Y."

"All right, so your sister's living full time with your dad, and Brian and anybody else in the house? Does your dad have a new girlfriend?"

"No."

"Wife or anything? Okay. Did he ever date much after your mom?"

"Not at all."

"Really?"

"Yeah."

"Wow," said Campion. "That's just devastating. Wow. Do you think that's related to what happened with your mom?"

"I don't know."

"What does your dad do for work?" Campion said. "Does he have a job?"

"No, he's on a disability claim. Used to be a plans checker for, um, I forget the company but it was down in Danville. And then he got too messed up to work."

"Like back issues?"

"Yeah. Back and neck issues."

"And neck?"

"He has a broken back that ruptured a bunch of disks. So he's got a bunch of titanium in his lower back basically."

"So he's had the surgery?"

"Yeah."

"I've been trying to avoid that," Campion said.

"And he broke his neck, so he has a bunch of, there too."

"Broke his neck? Like really had an accident?"

"Yeah, like it actually broke and he lived through it and so he's got a bunch of steel in them."

"Wow. Wow. How does he get along? I mean, that's got to be constant pain."

"Yeah, not very well. Uh, makes him pretty irritable. Uh, doesn't help with his temper, but he's on a lot of painkillers."

"Does he look like one of those guys that we have so many in our society right now that are just kind of addicted, you know, like Brett Favre, the football player?"

"Yeah."

"Would you say that's?"

"I'd say that both of my parents are addicted to painkillers."

"Oh, your mom too?" said Campion. "What's wrong with her? What's her issue?"

"Uh, she has fibromyalgia and trigeminal neuralgia, and she might have MS. They're not sure yet."

"One of those questionable diagnoses nobody really knows yet."

"MS takes like years to diagnose."

"Can, yeah. It might be a number of things, kind of in that family of diseases."

"Yeah," Marsh said.

"But is she still working right now?"

"Yeah."

"I think somebody said she works for the city here, right?"

"Yeah, she does."

"Yeah, I think so," said detective Pineda. Campion continued to pose the questions.

"Um, so she takes a lot of pain meds too, you said?"

"Yeah."

"Do you take any medications?"

"Um, I take anti-depressant, anti-anxiety, and a little bit of mood stabilizer."

"What, what are they?"

"Uh, Wellbutrin, Zoloft, and Abilify."

"Abilify?"

"Yeah."

"Isn't that mostly an anti-psychotic?"

"Yeah," Marsh said, "but they also add it on to anti-depressants to help with stuff that come along with depression. Helps with like you know, a little bit of mood swings, uh, helps with anxiety too. It just kind of calms you down."

"All right. So but you have had any, had psychotic, uh, psychosis type indicators?"

"Um, a while back but that was just kind of a mental break."

"What happened, Dan?"

"Um, I snapped mentally and I was scared that I was going to hurt myself or that I might hurt somebody else. I didn't feel safe, so I was put into a mental hospital in Sacramento for about week."

"Okay."

"But since then I've had no issues like that."

"Were you on any of those medications before this happened?"

"Um, no."

"Not on Zoloft?"

"No," Marsh said. "This is what kind of kick-started all of the getting me help and stuff."

"Do you get monitored? Are you, do you go in and talk to people about you know, counseling type stuff and get your blood levels taken?"

"Sure."

"Sure that they've got the right levels and stuff like that?"

"Yeah."

"And you do that in Sacramento as well?"

"No, I do that in Vacaville."

"In Vacaville?"

"The Kaiser in Vacaville."

"Okay. So and you have a doctor that supervising this?"

"Yeah."

"And going through?"

"I have a psychiatrist," Marsh said. "I have a doctor, who you know, prescribes medication and monitors it, and had a few blood tests taken, you know."

"Okay, because some of the, especially in teenagers, you probably know, I hope they would have told you anyways, some of the antidepressants have. . . ."

"Suicidal ideation that go along with it."

The teen's quick response impressed Campion.

"This kid is up on it," he said.

"How long have you been getting this help?" asked Pineda. "I think you mentioned before but I forget."

"Um, since December."

"Is that this past December?"

"Yeah."

"Is that when this happened, when you went to Sacramento?"

"Yeah, that's what kick-started it all. I think that's what we got it like, alright, 'he needs help.'"

Campion was curious.

"Can you talk to us a little but about it, Dan, about how you felt? I mean, what was the, what was the, your outlook on the world at this point?"

"I hated it."

"Yeah?"

"Um, my outlook on the world hasn't really changed, but my outlook on life has. I, at the time I thought it was, it was pointless, and there was no point in doing anything because you're just going to end up getting hurt and you're gonna die in the end anyways. There's uh, I didn't see a point in living."

"So your outlook on the world, you said hasn't changed, but that?"

"Yeah I . . ."

"Point of living, has that changed?"

"Yeah," Marsh said. "Um, I got to the point where I actually wake up in the mourning and I want to be alive, you know, like I want to experience what life has. You know, I mean, I'm 16, I've just started, got my whole life ahead of me, to experience all the things that there are to experience."

"That's true," Campion said. "I mean, you are very young, so I'm, what, what kind of got you to the point where you realized that you needed help? Usually that's a really hard thing."

"Um, it was one I became mentally broke and I was like, uh, I used to like harm myself."

"I see a scar or two there, yeah," Campion said. "Do you have a bunch? I think I can just see one or two."

"Not really that many. Just here."

"Oh, now I see closer, yeah."

"No, not at all, doesn't that?"

"It what?"

"No, this doesn't have anything to do with the suicide attempts."

"Okay, yeah. I recognized those. Can I see them a little closer? My eyes are getting old."

Campion touched Marsh's forearm.

"That doesn't hurt when I touch it, though, does it?"

"No, these are like really old."

"They're well healed," Campion said. "You just pulled back for a second. I'm curious."

"It was prior to that December two?" asked Pineda. "Is it really, really old?"

"Yeah," Marsh said. "This is like probably two years old."

"Okay," Campion said.

"I haven't done that in a long time, but when I had a really strong urge to, and I felt the way I did when I attempted suicide, and I don't know, I knew I wasn't safe where I was and I needed something to change. I knew that I couldn't expect to get better if I didn't start changing things and trying and wanting to get better, because you get to a point where it gets so bad that you don't even want to get better anymore."

"Yeah, usually that's why I was asking what changed," Campion said. "Because usually it's very hard for people that are as low down into the cycle as you're describing to on their own decide that they need help. Usually it's somebody else says, 'You need help.' And they bring them, bring you to somebody. Did somebody do that for you?"

"No. It was a voluntary hospitalization."

"But I mean, whose idea was it really?" said Campion. "Did somebody, like your mom or your dad?"

"No, it was me."

"Or the principal or somebody say, you know, 'You need to. . .' It was you?"

"No. I went to the school counselors and I was like, 'I need help.'"

"Wow," said Campion, as detective Pineda posed a question.

"Is this when you were mentioning earlier that you used the word or phrase 'rock bottom?'"

"Yeah."

"What was going on at that time that made it rock bottom?"

"I just, I don't know," Marsh said, "When nothing is done about clinical depression, over time, it's just gonna fester and get worse and worse. And at the time, you know, I didn't really have that many people in my life that I felt actually cared about me, you know, 'cause my dad threw me out. My mom, all she does is take her meds and work. Like we never had a genuine conversation, ever."

"Wow," said Campion.

"Um, my sister was moving out, so, well her and Brian were, it was just going to be me and my mom and I felt like I didn't really, I didn't really have anyone, and it wouldn't really matter if I was gone or not. And I don't know, I just, you get to a point where it's just, it's not necessarily that you want to die. It's just that you want the pain to stop."

"And has the pain stopped, Dan?"

"To an extent, um," Marsh said. "I'm not suicidal, but I'm still depressed. I still have those issues. They're just not nearly as severe as they were."

"God," said Campion. "I would have know that you were blowing sunshine up my skirt if you had said it stopped completely, because it doesn't."

"This?"

"I have a pretty good idea, but I'd like to hear it from you."

"Well, um, I actually had a pretty big eating disorder around the time that this happened. Um, and all the pain and depression and anger just like, I internalized it and I directed it towards myself. And honestly also I just kind of wanted to feel something. And well, I did."

"You did. Did it hurt?"

"It wasn't really pain," Marsh said. "It was just kind of a rush of like adrenaline, I guess. Uh, it was, I just wanted to feel something."

"So this was a couple of years ago?"

"Yeah."

"And I'm looking, you know. What did you do, the same spot over and over again?"

"Um, well, I did like, yeah. Seven here and seven here and I just kind of go over it."

"And what did you use?"

"Um, at first I used a broken mug."

"Whoa."

"Yeah. And then I started using a knife from the kitchen, and well, I eventually stopped because I was like, 'This is stupid.'"

"Where'd you get the idea?" Campion said. "Where, how did this occur to you?"

"Well, I don't know," Marsh said. "People at school, it seemed, had been cutting themselves. I had a girlfriend at the time who cut herself. I'd known people who had cut themselves, I'd heard about it. I figured, you know, never tried it, let's give it a shot, I guess. And I was like, it's not exactly the kind of attitude I'd want towards something like that."

"Well, I mean, you described pretty much what I've heard people describe who've done it as to why, you know, wanting to feel something."

"Yeah."

"You know," Campion said, "wanting to feel anything, even if it's pain, the adrenaline rush, like you said. Um, that's a big thing. And especially when you're depressed, of course that really, you need something to try and break out of that."

"Yeah."

"Um, your girlfriend at the time, what's her name?"

"Greta."

"Greta? And is she still in Davis here?"

"Yeah."

"Has she gotten help? I mean, is she . . ?"

"I don't know," Marsh said. "She, um, she pulled a lot of bullshit, so I completely backed away from that."

"She pulled bullshit regarding you? Or just in the school at large?"

"Uh, regarding me."

"Like what kind of stuff?"

"She, um, she cheated on me with a good friend of mine."

"Cheated," Campion said. "I'm sorry?"

"She cheated on me with somebody who was supposedly a good friend of mine."

"Really?"

"And, and she did it again with another of my friends, and by that point it's like, 'get the hell away from me.' Like, 'no, I'm done with this.'"

"How did you find out that she had cheated on you?"

"Um, she left a page open on the Internet."

"Accidentally?"

"Accidentally, and that was how I found out about the first one."

"What, what page was it?"

"On Facebook."

"Facebook?" Campion said. "His Facebook?"

"Um, no, it was like her and she had her message open to him and that was that. And the second . . ."

"What was in the message, Dan? Do you remember?"

"Not exactly," Marsh said, "but I remember they were being really flirty and they were talking about like when they met up and I don't know, I don't want to go into detail. When they fooled around, I guess and, I don't know. I've had that happen to me a few times, and each time it's like, it's complete betrayal of trust."

"Complete betrayal," Campion said. "And it makes it hard to trust other people then going forward, right?"

"Well, yeah."

"Once you've figured out okay, I got to stay away from Greta, but then you know you meet somebody else. So you said it's happened more than once?"

"Yes."

"Since Greta?"

"No, not since."

"Okay, after," Campion said. "Do you see her? Is she still in school?"

"Uh, I haven't seen her since we broke up."

"Oh, really? How long ago was that?"

"Probably like a little over a year ago."

"Okay. How big is Davis High School? I guess I don't know. How many student are there?"

"Like 2,000."

"Okay," Campion said. "So I guess you could go for a year without seeing somebody at school or she go to the continuation school or anything? Is there more than one high school in Davis?"

"No, I was one year ahead of her."

"Oh, okay."

"And since and Davis ninth grade and tenth grade get separated. We broke up when I was in the ninth grade, and so I went to the high school and she stayed where she was, and so I haven't seen her since."

"I see. Well, what grade are you in now?"

"I'm going into like my junior year."

"So you'll start eleventh grade, okay, so you finished tenth grade. Got you. All right. Well, that is, that is very hard to deal with that kind of betrayal of, you know, trust. And especially what happened to your dad, you know."

"Yeah."

"Having that betrayal by your mom."

"Well, it's like, that happened when I was a kid," Marsh said, "so that already you know effects like, oh, wow, I can't really trust people. And then like growing up, uh, my sister had a lot of boyfriends and she would cheat on them. And it's like, okay, wow, I really can't trust people. And then the first girlfriend cheated on me like three times, I come to find out later. And it's like, all right, really you can't trust people. And then the next one did it and the next one did it and the next one did it."

"Damn. Wow."

"So, it's like, wow, you guys really keep proving me right. Quit it. I don't like being right about that."

"Do you think that there was some element of having that happen with your mom?" Campion said. "Does that, how does that effect how you react to it, do you think?"

"Um, I think it makes it even more painful, because part of me just like regresses back to when I saw that happen, and when all that happens, so then the pain of what had just happened and then it like kind of picks up the scab. And I don't know, it's, um, every time it just kind of devastates me, 'cause it's like again, really? Are you kidding me? Come on?"

"Can I catch one break?"

"Yeah, seriously."

"I'm not going to go into platitudes about how it happens to all of us. Even if it does or did, you know, it still hurts like hell."

"Yeah."

"What other hurts you got in your life?"

"Oh, I've got a whole plethora of hurts."

That got a rise out of the FBI man.

"Plethora," he said. "You don't hear that word worked into conversation too often. What are the, what's in the plethora, in the bouquet of Dan's hurts?"

"Well, this one's not really much of a hurt, more of a trauma," Marsh said. "When I was taking care of my mom when she had, she basically had to stay in bed. She was bedridden the whole time while she, before she had her brain surgery to help with her fibromyalgia and her trigeminal neuralgia. She'd have seizures like several times a week."

"Uh-huh."

"And so I'd have to like hold my mom and like get her through these seizures and watching that happen, you know. Each time it's kind of scary. Cause its like, you know, you made it last time, but what if you don't this time."

"And it's your mom."

"Yeah."

"I mean, it should be her taking care of you."

"I mean, I don't have the best relationship, but it's still my mom."

"She had an actual surgery, huh?"

"Yeah, she had brain surgery."

"What did they do to her brain?"

"Um, they like cauterized the trigeminal nerve that was messing with the side of her face, and so that got better, and then she got it on this side, so now she has it again."

"Hmm."

"So I don't know," Marsh said. "That kind of screws with your head, constantly seeing, and holding your mom through seizures. Um, someone who was very close to me and would help me through a lot of that, you know, when my parents got split up and everything was happening, was around for a few years and two years ago he died."

"Hm."

"And I, I don't know, um. I don't have many people in my life that I genuinely care about or genuinely care about me, so when I lose someone like that, it's, it's hard."

"What's his name?"

"Boris."

"Boris?" Campion said. "And he lived in Davis here?"

"Yeah."

"How did you know him?"

"Um, he worked with my mom, and he came over once and we started talking. It just kind of built from there."

"He worked with your mom, you said you know, at the city as well, and adult male, all that kind of stuff?"

"Yeah," Marsh said.

"But a good guy?"

"Yeah."

"And so he would be there to talk to you about things, and like surrogate father?"

"Yeah, pretty much."

"Is that going too far?" Campion said.

"Uh, me and dad never had a father-son relationship, like we never really had those in-depth conversations or those building milestones. We never did anything together. We never went out and did things. With Boris it was like, he'd, we'd talk about, well, everything that was going on, have really deep conversations and we'd to out to like sporting events, like football games and stuff."

"And he's not there for you anymore. What happened to him? How did he pass away?"

"Um, well, he took uh, medication with alcohol and didn't wake up."

"Did he commit suicide, Dan?"

"I don't know," Marsh said. "I really don't. I don't know if he was just not thinking or whether he killed himself."

"Did he ever talk to you about suicide?"

"No, but."

"The topic never came up between the two of you?"

"Well, he never talked to me about him being suicidal."

"He talked about it with you," Campion said. "But did you talk to him about your own feelings?"

"Yeah, but uh, never actually. I wasn't suicidal at the time, and he didn't give me any indications that he was, either."

"So this was two years ago, and so that really hadn't started happening when you're 13, 14 years old yet?"

"Yeah."

"Or it had?"

"It uh, it was kind of when it, things started to get worse," Marsh said. "It started to head in that direction, but wasn't quite there yet."

"Okay."

"And then you know, losing someone like that kind of speeds up that train."

"That sharp downward decline."

"Yeah."

"Well, did you ever have a plan for suicide or were you there at, close enough that you actually thought about how you would do it?"

"Yeah," Marsh said, "I, I attempted it four times in my life."

"So the attempts were what?"

"And each time made it, uh, one of them I just went on this massive drinking binge and tried to drink myself to death."

"All at once?"

"Yeah, uh, I was drinking like a handle of vodka or whisky every day for like two weeks straight."

"Wow."

"I was wondering, you know, how much of this can I take already, come on. I, yeah, it was bad."

"What else?" said Campion. "What other things did you think about doing or planned to do? What were the attempts?"

"I tried to OD on morphine," Marsh said, "and well, I just woke up in a pile of puke. So that didn't work out. Uh, the eating disorder, I tried to starve myself to death, to within a week or two of dying, then saved, so that didn't work out. And then this one just like fucking odd, so that we're going this way, I went with like something that, you know, this has to work. I was gonna get run over by a train. And so I was lying down on the train tracks waiting for it to come. And it starts, you know I hear it coming, it gets closer and closer, and then it switches tracks and goes to the one that I'm not on and just misses me by like ten seconds."

"Wow," said Campion.

"And at that point I was like, okay, screw this."

"It's not meant to be."

"Yeah, seriously," Marsh said. "If I'm not, if I can't die then I'm just gonna give up trying."

"So if you, uh, was anybody with you or around at any of those?"

"No."

"The cutting, did you ever do that with anybody?"

"No."

"With Greta or anybody else, any other friends?"

"No, I never," Marsh said. "I knew it was wrong. I know it was messed up and I didn't want to have the people around me doing it too."

"So you would do it by yourself?"

"Yeah."

"And did your mom ever find out about it, or your dad?"

"No."

"Anybody that's supposed to be taking care of you, looking after you, protecting you?" Campion said. "And how about the suicide attempts? They didn't find out either? Never told them later?"

"No."

"Did you ever tell Boris, or was that before?"

"No, this was before."

"That was before. Um, alright."

Detective Pineda asked if anybody needed a break. Campion turned to Marsh.

"Okay. You good? Water, okay, bathroom, anything?"

"I'm good," Marsh said, but he wasn't done.

"Um, what exactly are you guys trying to get from me?"

Chapter 5

"I'm a compassionate, affectionate person."

"Well, here's where kind of concerns are Dan," Campion said. "People who are much more tech savvy than me because I'm just an old guy, I don't know anything about anything, found this thing called Tumblr, and your Tumblr page. Is that the right term?"

"Yeah."

"Yeah," Campion said. "Tell me about that. How did that come to be?"

"Tumblr? Um, I heard about it, I made one."

"Okay. So describe to me the stuff that's on there."

"On my page, or on Tumblr in general?"

"On your, on your page, yeah."

"Um, song lyrics, uh, things like minutia things about like what I feel. A lot of stuff from horror movies, 'cause I like horror movies, um, gore. That's pretty much it, just music and scary stuff."

"Horror movies and gore, yeah."

"Yeah."

"It seems like there's a lot of that on there."

"Since I was a little kid I liked horror movies. I've been watching them for a long time and, uh, I don't get grossed out by gore."

"I'm wondering if it is a refuge for you, Dan?"

"In a way, kind of is, um. I've got a dark, screwed-up sense of humor, and actually a lot of that stuff makes me laugh when I see it, and I don't know, not a lot of stuff makes me laugh."

"Hm."

"And so it's like, I like horror movies, and so it's just, it's the same thing as a horror movie only it's real. Since I don't have any connection to whoever did happened to, it really doesn't bother me."

"Right," Campion said. "So and it's kind of like the cutting. It's a feeling, right?"

"Yeah, seriously. Like it makes me feel something, and I'm just always kind of been into darker stuff."

"And what do you feel? When you say it makes you feel something, what is it that you're feeling when you see the, the stuff on Tumblr, the gore?"

"I don't know," Marsh said. "It makes me kinda like shocked and I don't know. I'm fascinated with anatomy, and so I, um, you can see what happened to them and how warped their bodies are and just kind of fascinating to think like, what could have done that? How did that happen? Um, why did that happen? Just how did this all come to play, and I don't know. Sometimes they'll be like in a funny pose or something and it's just look right, like stupid, and so I'll like giggle at it."

"Kind of makes you feel something."

"Yeah."

"And it gives you a, a feeling, right?" Campion said. "A little momentary burst of, of funniness or joy?"

"I don't know if it's really joy," Marsh said. "It's just kind of a feeling."

"A feeling. That's interesting."

"Yeah. It's not negative, it's not super positive, it's just kind of . . .'

"A giggle, a yuck."

"I guess."

"I mean that, I'm not putting words in your mouth, but I'm just trying to understand."

"Yeah, I guess that'd be, uh. What's the concern with that, though? It's Tumblr."

"It is, and you know, I know that there's all those websites out there like, bestgore.com and I mean, what are some, what are some of the other ones that you know about?"

"That's the only one I know about," Marsh said.

"Bestgore and, and that one's got a lot of stuff on it."

"Yeah."

"So yeah, that's, I mean it's dark, like you say."

"Well, it's also a lot of stuff that's like, it's relevant to what's going on today. Like there's, a lot of it is just, um, stuff that's happening in Syria, and it's like, holy crap, this is actually going on right now and no one's doing anything about it. And I don't know, I like horror movies, so it's just kind of like a real life horror movie."

"Mm-hm."

"I don't really make the distinction."

"Yeah and years ago on those sites they would have, uh, things that the folks would post from Iraq."

"Yeah."

"You know, of the U.S. soldiers being killed and stuff like that, and that was, you know. . ."

"It's brutal and it's dark," Marsh said, "but it's interesting to me."

"And you said anatomy. You said you had an interest in anatomy. Tell me a little about that."

"Well, just the human body is fascinating," Marsh said. "It's crazy how it can all work the way it does, how it's always just set up and connected. It's always just relevant. The brain controls everything. I don't know, it's really cool."

"So your brain tells you to move your hand like that, to turn it over."

"Yeah, and like um, I've got like kind of bony hands, so I can like see my tendons and stuff."

"Yeah."

"So I just find it fascinating to like see what, what's on the inside, you know. Like not just this, 'cause what makes it all happen, what makes it work, what it is."

"Right," Campion said. "So that, that's part of the fascination with the gore stuff?"

"Yeah."

"Bestgore? Um, 'cause yeah, I mean, that's all laid open. But I mean, if you were interested in that, there's stuff like anatomy textbooks, and things like that. Do you have any of that kind of stuff?"

"Yeah, I do, um. My mom has a couple of anatomy textbooks that I look through."

"Okay. Okay," Campion said. "So it's an unusual Tumblr page and it reflects your interest. It's the window to your soul. I did notice, too, some other things, though, Dan, about some real vulnerable things for you."

"Well, yeah, I mean, I've got a dark sense of humor and, and a messed up person but I'm still human, still have feelings."

"Yeah. And that comes through, that kind of reflection that come through that you are a person who wants, who wants contact. You want to be . . ."

"Well, yeah."

"Embraced."

"Whether, every human being whether they're consciously aware of it or not, is just seeking affection. They want somebody to just emotionally connect with."

"Okay, I agree," Campion said. "That's what most human behavior is all about."

"Yeah."

"Most all of it."

"Like, the way I see it the reason we're here is to help see each other through life, whatever we are going through."

"Yeah, and that's a big part of my purpose," Campion said. "So I am not sure how far you and Ariel talked about what kind of led us to you, and to kind of look into Dan and everything about Daniel."

"He just said that like, he heard a rumor or something. He didn't really tell me why me. He just kind of asked me those stereotypical questions, you know, like where were you, who were you with, what do you know?"

"Okay," said Campion. "So the rumors that he's referring to are people saying specific things about what you have told other people."

"Well, what?" Marsh said. "What would that be?"

"That, you were there. That you did those murders."

"Me?"

"Mm-hm."

"That's ridiculous."

"Why is it ridiculous?"

"I'm a kid."

"No, that's. . ."

"Well, like, I don't, I don't hurt people. Like, you can ask anyone around me. I'm a compassionate, affectionate person. I care about people. I don't wanna hurt them. I mean, yeah, they piss me off sometimes and they do some messed-up shit, but I care about people."

"I know there's probably some people that you do care about," Campion said, "and as far as being a kid, Dan, I mean, least year I was, or last week, last month, sorry about that one. I was up in Calaveras County. Did you ever see anything in the news about that, about a 12-year-old boy who murdered his sister? He stabbed her to death in their house."

"Really?"

"Mm-hm, and tried to make it look like an intruder had done it."

"That's intense."

"It is," Campion said. "It's intense. I see you as a person who has a need. You have a big need. You have a need for refuge, maybe more than anybody I've ever run across. At age 16, just 16, that's remarkable. I don't know if that's a good thing, probably not, but it is an unusual thing to see, to meet a person like you, Dan, who has been through some of the things you have and has this need, the compulsion, I think the need to do something, to feel."

"Well, yeah," Marsh said. "But I don't hurt people. I don't."

"Dan, the information that was said, that came out of your mouth, had specifics of what happened in that house, of those two elderly people, that only the person who was inside that house would know. Very specific information."

"I, what?" Marsh said. "I said that someone broke in and stabbed the people?"

"Yeah. No, what we're picking up on is that you said to other people who may have repeated it to other people is information that is so specific, not just that somebody broke in and stabbed two people, but exactly what was done to those people."

"Well, have you asked the people who have told you that?"

"Where they were?"

"Well, I mean, when someone comes to you and tells you exact details of a murder and then says, no, this guy did it, isn't that kind of like . . ."

"Like we should think about that, that maybe he was there, she was there or?"

"Yeah, or that maybe he . . ."

"Whoever is telling us?"

"Is trying to screw me over? I mean, my best friend is really fucking up my life right now. My ex-best friend."

"Who, who are you referring to?" Campion said. "Your ex-best friend?"

"Alvaro Garibay."

"Okay."

"Um, I don't know," Marsh said. "It seems like he has vendetta out for me or something."

"What is that based on?"

"I don't know, what, give me what his reason of what's my reason to say that?"

"Why, why do you think he has a vendetta against you?"

"Well, like, he knew I carried a knife," Marsh said, "and he never had a problem with it, until one day he randomly reported me to the office and started all of this. You know, got me arrested and put in the system for a misdemeanor, got me most likely expelled from the high school. And I asked him why, and he said 'I don't like you and I don't want you here.'"

"Okay."

"And it's like, why would you do that? I don't know, um, and also me and my girlfriend broke up about a week and a half ago, and now he's trying to get with her."

"Alvaro is?"

"Yeah," Marsh said. "And he's talking crap about me to friends, telling people to stay away from me and I'm a bad influence and I'm weird. That just, I don't know what it is. I've never done anything to him, and I don't know why he's trying to fuck me over."

"I don't know if that's who it is or not," Campion said. "I don't know who, who is the person who actually brought this to the attention of the police department. I have no idea, but I think it's more than one person and I think that it is so specific, Dan, that the person who said it, which more than one person is saying is you, were there, beyond any possibility of a doubt. Nothing that was in the newspaper, nothing that's publicly known. Half the people around this police station don't even know the details that were being brought forth there. It is just a certainty."

"Well, yeah, but . . ."

"Is Alvaro the kind of guy who could do something like that?"

"Yeah."

"How so?"

"He's killed animals before," Marsh said. "I've seen him choke a cat to death."

"Yeah."

"Seen him abuse his dog violently."

"In what kind of way?"

"Beating it, kicking it, choking it."

"Dan," Campion said. "People have told us that's the kind of stuff you do, too."

"I don't."

"You never hurt an animal?"

"Not intentionally. I've gotten mad and I've like, I've hit my dog but. . ."

"Like kicked your dog?"

"Yeah."

"Choked your dog?"

"No, not choked, kicked it cause it's you know, it's annoying," Marsh said. "It ran into me. It won't shut up, it's just like stop. But I don't intentionally harm animals."

"Cats, are there kind of any other animals?"

"No. I, you can ask my mom. I've always loved animals. I, I never intentionally harmed one, other, well, you know, like hit it, but that's a disciplinary thing, not as an abusive thing."

"That's the only time?"

"Yeah."

"But Alvaro has?" Campion said. "That's what you are telling us?"

"Yeah."

"So that if we talked to everybody that Alvaro knows and everybody who's close to him, and everybody that's close to you, Dan, and everybody who would know, people are gonna say, Dan doesn't do anything like that to animals, but Alvaro does?"

"I don't know if they'd say that he does, but is he, me and him were like, we were brothers, you know. We told each other everything. We like, I don't know if he's told other people about it."

"So he told it to you, or did you see it?"

"He told me and I saw some of it."

"I saw him choke a cat to death and I saw him beat the hell out of his dog."

"When, when he choked the cat to death, who else was there? Was there anybody else there?"

"It was just me."

"And where were you guys?"

"We were out by um, Playfield Park," Marsh said. "It's by his house and there was just this stray cat and I don't know, he just said 'Come here and watch this.' Starts choking it. Oh, okay."

"And then what happened?"

"He just kept choking it. It started flailing and squirming and he just wouldn't stop."

"And what eventually happened with the cat then?"

"Well, it stopped moving."

"And what did he do with it?"

"He threw it in the trash can."

"Was there any cutting on the cat," Campion said. "Any exploration?"

"Not that I'm aware of. I don't know. It's the kind of thing that's like, you can't really stop him 'cause he's like, your brother, he's your best friend, but it's fucked up."

"Well, you know, probably, because you're a smart guy and, there's a high correlation between people who have certain physiologically, neurologically interesting brain development, you know, the kind of white matter thing like your principal was talking about. But they get that and that's where their head's at. That's what they like to do. That's where that compulsion leads them, that obsession. So are you telling me that Alvaro's that kind of guy?"

"I am," Marsh said. "He, he doesn't come off as it, but he's really a fucked-up kid. He's got a bad past. He was abused. He told me that he started hurting animals when he was a kid."

"Like how old?"

"Like seven or eight. I don't know. I know that he's capable of some messed-up shit."

"Like what else?" Campion said.

"I think anyone who can hold down another like living being, stare into its eyes and kill it, uh, they're capable of more."

"Like what?"

"They're capable of killing," Marsh said.

"Yeah, well, that's what you've described is they would be killing that animal, that other living being. And that's what I'm saying. Sometimes that's where people get in their lives, where that's the only refuge they have. That's the only way they can feel. That's the only way they can feel alive. And starting when you're eight or nine, that's absolutely, having that experimentation with, with animals is where it starts. People that I've seen, mostly guys I've seen later in life, but it can happen and it does happen, and it did happen here in Davis."

"Like yeah, sorry," Marsh said.

"If it did happen that Alvaro was involved in, in killing these two older people, what should happen to him?"

"He should go to jail."

"Okay," Campion said. "You know in, in California, you know I don't know how old he is. Is he a juvenile too?"

"He's 17."

"He's 17. So you know, juvenile hall, do you know anything about that?"

"Um, not a lot."

"Have you ever been?"

"No," Marsh said. "This whole knife thing on campus is the first any sort of negative interaction I've had with authority, with the law."

"Has Alvaro had any?"

"I don't know. Um, he used to take family trips to Mexico and he's told me stories of like him and his cousins would do stupid shit. They'd like to play games where they'd like um, fucking shoot the neighbor's animals with fireworks. They'd drive around and do stupid crap. I don't know, he's done reckless, dumb crap and I don't know."

"Did he ever tell you that he was involved in these murders in Davis here?"

"No," Marsh said, "but he brought it up to me a few times."

"Like what?"

"Like he asked me if I'd heard about it and like what did I think about it and stuff like that."

"And when would this have been?"

"Mmm, probably within the week that it happened."

"The week or so after it happened a couple of months ago?"

"Yeah," Marsh said. "Like that you know when it made the news and everyone was, I don't know, he kept bringing it up to me."

"Okay."

"I didn't really think anything of it."

Campion kept up the pace.

"So if he's bringing this up a week or two afterwards and didn't say that he was involved with it and you guys are like brothers, and now two months later, either he or somebody he said something to or down the chain, you know, then he said to, you know, somebody else who said something to somebody else and brings it to the police, wherever the chain is. I don't know where, or even if it was him. But how does it come back to you then? You were the one who had these, these very intimate details of what happened."

"I don't know," Marsh said. "I don't know anything about it other than what I've told you. I don't know what it is but I really think he's trying to screw me over, 'cause he didn't apologize for turning me in for the knife or anything. He just told me he doesn't want anything to do with me."

"This is your best friend."

"And he doesn't want to. Yeah, he was."

"What happened between the two of you?"

"I don't know," Marsh said. "This is out of nowhere."

"And the knife thing happened not that long ago, right?"

"Yeah, on May 28th I think."

"So what happened to change your relationship?" Campion said. "You said something about a girlfriend."

"Yeah. I don't know if that had anything to do with it. I'm really not sure why he did that. That's why I'm shocked and appalled, like out of nowhere he just decided to stab me in the back and cut me off."

"With the knife thing, turning it in to the school, turning you in to the school?"

"Yeah."

"But is there a girlfriend involved? You, you made some reference of a girlfriend."

"Yeah."

"That either was your girlfriend . . ."

"Yeah."

"Or?"

"Uh, me and her were going and her and him were also friends, and like they'd hang out. And now me and her broke up, and now they're hanging out and he's like trying to get with her."

"What's her name, his girlfriend's name?"

"Sally."

"Sally. What's her last name?"

Marsh spelled it out, along with Alvaro's.

"All right," Campion said. "So is she, are you in contact with her?"

"Um, up until a few days ago, she told me that um, like since we broke up, she told me that we need to stop being in contact if we want to get over it, you know."

"When did you, um, break up?"

"Uh, the fifth of June."

"The fifth of June?"

"Yeah."

"So pretty recently."

"Yeah."

"And what, what happened?"

"Uh, she's just, she said she's too mentally screwed up to be in a relationship right now and she is. She's got horrible depression, um, she sees things, like she's seriously she might be a schizophrenic and so am I, 'cause she has, she literally sees things happened around her. Like she'll see something that isn't there."

"Mm-hm."

"She hates herself beyond belief," Marsh said. "She has a really bad, had a really bad self-form problem, terrible body image issues, just such of an intense self-hatred, like something unlike I've ever seen."

"Even more than your own?"

"Yeah and. . ."

"Which is saying something."

"Yeah. And she's just too messed up to be in a relationship right now. And I get that, you know, if you need to take care of yourself first, like you got to make sure you're okay before you can try and help other people to be okay, too, you know. At least make it so you can actually do something to help."

"Yeah. Yeah, she would have to be," Campion said. "So but did she get in the relationship with Alvaro after that?"

"No, they're not going out."

"I thought I understood you said that, that they were in some kind of . . ."

"No, he's trying to get at her, not go out with her."

"He, oh, what do you mean get at her?"

"Like fuck her."

"Oh," Campion said. "Have sex."

"I'm being blunt."

"Yeah, that's fine," Campion said. "Okay. So he wants to but does she want to? You don't know."

"I don't know."

"Recently she told you that it's best if you guys don't have any contact. Did something happen in particular?"

"No," Marsh said. "Nothing happened."

"When was the last time you saw her?"

"I don't know. Like three or four days ago."

"And how did, what was the context of that?"

"Well, I went to go see her in Dixon, and we just, we talked for a really long time about you know, how we're feeling, what we want to happen, where I want this to end up. And that was the last time I saw her."

"Had you been intimate with her, Dan? Had you had sex with her?"

"Yeah."

"And when was the last time that you guys had sex?"

"Like a month ago."

"So before June five?"

"Yeah."

"Okay, had she gone back and forth on you at all with anything? I want you, I don't want you, any of that kind of stuff?"

"Yeah. Um, she says she loves me and she really wants to be with me, but she can't because the way she is now she's hurting herself and hurting me because, the way she put it is she loves me so much that when she hurts me, it hurts her, and she was, she was doing a lot of stupid shit, and so it hurt me, and messed with me."

"What kind of stupid shit?"

"Uh, going out at night at like three in the morning with a bunch of people to go get high and like wander around town uh, getting drunk with groups of people. I don't know, she's just, she's acting really stupid."

"So risky behavior, risky stuff?"

"Yeah," Marsh said, "And stuff that like I told her I'm not okay with at all, and she did it anyways. And so that in turn hurt me and which apparently hurts her and with all the shit already going on with her, she can't take it anymore."

"Do you feel like she understands you?"

"Yeah."

"Sounds like you guys have a lot. . ."

"I think to a pretty good extent, yeah."

"How long were you guys together?"

"Six months."

"Six months since before June first, so like right around the first of the year?"

"Yeah, uh, we got together on December fourth."

"So that was before the, um, you went to Sacramento and admitted yourself."

"Yeah."

"Okay. Was that related?"

"No."

"Okay. Dating her didn't kind of make you realize that you wanted to take care of things and get some help?"

"Well, in a way, but mainly I was doing it for myself."

Campion listened, paused, and gathered his thoughts.

"Okay," he said. "Well, we have this, this issue then. We still have this problem, Dan, and it's a big problem because somebody knows a lot of information and stuff that only somebody who was there is gonna know. And we look at that and we look at your Tumblr page and we look at everything that I understand about people in your position that I've met along the way in the 25 years in doing this, and people are saying, 'that's Dan, that's Dan, and he did it and here's why.'"

Chapter 6

"I'm just a scapegoat."

"I didn't do it," Marsh said. "I never killed anyone. I don't want to."

"Like you said, there's people that matter to you, but your curiosity, the graphic stuff, the graphic nature, just the attraction to that. How could you not? It's an obsession. It would be an obsession. It would be a compulsion."

"I could never do that to someone. I've gotten in fights out of self-defense."

"Yeah, I know," Campion said. "This is something completely different."

"Never, could I do that."

"This is a, this is a compulsion, Dan. Like we were talking about before, this is something where you can't help it. It's an obsession. You think about it all the time."

"Mm-hm."

"And after you're done with it, you're gonna feel a complete relief, a release, and you know, a feel. You feel. And you almost got away with it, I mean, that's the thing. I mean, the, the crime was a masterpiece of just technique."

"I didn't do it."

"It was a work of art, Dan."

"Okay."

"So?"

"Somebody did a good job."

Campion pondered the statement.

"You were very close to getting away with it," the FBI man said.

"Except for maybe a betrayal. Someone that you trusted then talked to somebody else, and that betrayal leads back to your whole life. I mean, since you were nine years old."

"Just cause I got a messed up life, and because I like scary movies and I like graphic content doesn't mean I'm a murderer."

"No, the thing that means. . ."

"Depression," Marsh said.

"The thing that means that you're a murderer, Dan, is because only the person who was inside there would know."

"Yeah, but I didn't tell you that."

"What was done to the person afterward," Campion said. "Other people said that you told them, and that's were we're at. So there's two roads. You know, you can go down the road of saying, wasn't me, I could never do that, and we're gonna talk to everybody you know, and we already are. And they're telling us, since you're talking about the cat, for example, that wasn't Alvaro, that was you."

"No," Marsh said. "It wasn't."

"The things that, that obsession, that, the thing that we see, and people again who are older than you usually. You're very young for this to have the onset of this, to start at eight or nine, is extremely young."

"What started at that age is my depression."

"Right," Campion said. "I'm not saying that it's not related to that. It, it's completely related to that, Dan. It's intertwined. It, it's almost one. And that, that depression and that, that self-loathing and that just life sucks, it all goes together, and you get to the point where you don't feel. You don't feel."

"The only person I've ever even attempted to kill is myself," Marsh said. "If I was gonna kill somebody it would be me."

"But Dan, the ways that you've tried to kill yourself are not the traditional ways that are simple and effective. Maybe the train, but even that is, is not the way that we usually see people who kill themselves."

"How is that relevant?"

"Because I don't think you wanted to kill yourself. I think you felt like there was no way around it, that you'd rather not be here, but you hadn't decided that you were gonna kill yourself completely."

"I, I did, though," Marsh said. "I was within a week of death when I was hospitalized. I took like 20 morphine pills."

"Look," Campion said. "You're cutting yourself to feel. You know how people cut themselves to drain all the blood out of their body, right?"

"Yeah."

"Overdosing on pills, getting a firearm and shooting themselves. Those are the ways that we see people committing suicide. And I'm not saying that that's really even that relevant. I know you were in pain. I know you were feeling horrible, and I think this is a refuge, like we talked about at the beginning. This is the refuge of the only thing that you can do that makes you feel alive."

"That was me over one year ago," Marsh said. "I've gotten better since then. I feel. I mean. . ."

"But we were talking about, you know, December, when you checked yourself in, right?"

"Yeah, since then I've gotten so much better. I've, I've experienced happiness. I've experienced all these feelings. I forgot what they felt like."

"What made you happy?"

"I figure it's a combination of anti-depressants and at the time I had a best friend who was really great to me and a girlfriend who was really great to me."

"And that made you happy?"

"Yeah."

"Do you think it's possible that they did it together," said Campion, "and that they're trying to blame you? Is that what you're saying?"

"No. What I'm saying is that's what made me happy."

"So you felt happy with them, but if, if it's in fact them, that is, starting this chain reaction of very specific information, you told me that whoever did that is the people we should be looking at, or the person we should be looking at."

"Well, I mean," Marsh said, "when someone comes to you with explicit details about a crime that no one knows, would know except the person who did it, shouldn't maybe they be a pretty big suspect?"

"It would occur to us, yes. It would occur to us to take a look at them, too, Dan."

"Rumors are just rumors."

"Right. And that's why we do an investigation and that's what we're doing. So there's a lot of stuff going on right now. There's searching being done. There are a lot of things going on. There's interviews going on. There's people being talked to. And we're going to find out what really happened. And what I'd like to do is to hear it from you and hear why, because the why is everything. And if I'm right, if I'm even close to being right about this as refuge for you, then I'd like to hear the why. And I want to give you that opportunity."

"You're asking the wrong person," Marsh said.

"Because I want to heal that person, Dan. I want to heal you."

"I am being healed. I, you're asking me to confess to something that I've never done and to tell you why I did it, but I've never done it."

"Do you see why it would be better for you to explain why you did it than just to say, it wasn't me, it wasn't me, even though the evidence starts mounting up? Do you understand that?"

"I understand how it would be better," Marsh said, "but I can't tell you why I did something that I didn't do."

"And you understand the whole difference between the juvenile, the prosecution where you will possibly get out when you're 25, or you will get out when you're 25 at the very latest, or a crime being prosecuted as an adult, which would have much more serious consequences in terms of time that somebody would be put away as an adult. And at age 15, 16, um, you're kind of in between. It could go either way. I would really hate to see somebody who has had so much happen to them in their life and so many reasons to do something, to feel that, to not explain it so that we can understand it. That's what we're here for, Dan."

"I can't explain to you something that I didn't do. I know people are saying that it was me, but that doesn't mean that it was me. I know I've got a screwed up past, but that doesn't mean it was me."

"The person who knew those details was in there," Campion said, "but they got everything right, and they did a textbook job. I mean, we literally had no clue. But we're gonna have some now. We're gonna have a lot of clues, 'cause we know where to look."

"Somebody in our circle did it, obviously, but I swear to you it wasn't me."

"Don't swear to me," Campion said, raising the volume a notch.

"Don't swear to me. I want to understand. I think I'm pretty close to understanding. I want to heal. I want to help."

"You're not hearing me when I say that I can't confess to something and tell you why I did something if I never did it."

Campion allowed a brief pause.

"We've been talking a long time today, and one of the things over 25 years I've gotten pretty good at is reading body language, and you see things on TV shows and all that kind of stuff about poker players, you know, of all the things can read faces and tells. You know what that is?"

"Yeah."

"You're not telling me the truth now, Dan."

"Wouldn't you be kind of freaked out if you already had anxiety and social anxiety and you're brought in here and people are accusing you of killing people?"

"It has nothing to do with being freaked out," Campion said. "It has to do with what I can see when you're telling the truth and when you're not. And I know when you're telling the truth and when you're not. And you're not telling me the truth now, Dan."

"I am," Marsh said. "I didn't kill anybody. I've never killed anyone before. I don't want to kill anyone. I don't want to hurt anyone."

"The person who did this will do it again," Campion said. "I have no doubt about it. They can't not. It's the obsession, it's the compulsion."

"Well, then maybe that's where you'll find your guy," Marsh said. "Sir, it's not me."

"So if there is one person and you're saying it's not you, in this circle of people that you deal with, who is it going to be?"

"I don't know."

"Is it going to be one or more than one person?"

"I don't know," Marsh said. "I have no idea. All I know about this murder is what I've told you. I don't know who did it. I don't know why they're trying to screw me over I don't know anything about this. And I don't know what you're trying to get me to say, 'cause I can't say that I did it when I didn't do it."

"I don't want you to say that you did it if you didn't do it," Campion said. "I want you to tell me why you did it."

"But I can't 'cause I didn't do it. I can't tell you why I did something that I didn't do."

"And you have no information about it? Alvaro never told you about it, your girlfriend never said anything about it to you?"

"No, they've never said that."

"You weren't there?"

"People have brought it up to me. That's it."

"But not specifics?"

"No."

"Think, did anybody," Campion said. "I'm asking you a question. Did anybody tell you that they did it?"

"No."

"Were you there when someone else did it?"

"No."

"Okay."

"I had nothing to do with it," Marsh said. "It's just a bunch of . . ."

"If it was just teenagers talking about some rumors and, and trying to, you know, get you in trouble, we'd be done, Dan, but it's not that. It's people who know what happened inside that house because they were there."

"Then you should ask those people."

"And they are saying that you did it."

"If the only people who knew that information are the ones who did it, then you have people telling you the information."

"Then we, we will and we would consider that they did it, but think about it for a second."

"I'm just a scapegoat," Marsh said.

Campion briefly pondered the term before moving on.

"Why would, if there was nothing that was indicating and pointing back towards them, because this was a very well executed crime. This is something that we see not that often, somebody who planned this out, carried it out meticulously. Why would they bring attention on themselves in order to blame you for it, if they were the ones who in fact did it? Because they would know that we would be looking at them."

"I don't know."

"It doesn't make any sense."

"It doesn't have to," Marsh said. "People don't make any sense."

"People at large don't make any sense but people do things that are usually in their own interest, and doing this would make no sense for them."

"Telling anybody that they did it wouldn't make any sense."

"No, not if you could avoid it, if you could avoid it, yes, I agree. But sometimes you just can't, because it's your refuge, because it's, it's where you felt alive. And it's just like the cutting and, and it's you – she told you about it, right?"

"Who?"

"Greta, correct?"

"Yeah."

"She told you about it and then you did it, right?"

"No, I've heard about it from tons of people."

"From other people," Campion said. "So she told you about that, right? Other people tell you about it. It's kind of the same thing. You're sharing it with your friends who you think are like-minded."

"I can't confess to something that I didn't do," Marsh said. "I can't tell you why I did something that I didn't do."

"I don't want you to. I want you to tell us why it happened."

"I don't know why it happened. I really don't."

"Okay. So going forward, would you agree that we've given you every opportunity to explain what happened and why, if in fact you would want to do that?"

"Um, yeah."

"Would that be fair to say?"

"Yeah, you've asked me to do that."

"We've given you every opportunity."

"Well, yeah, but I can't take advantage of an opportunity that . . ."

"Okay," Campion said. "So you've, you've had the opportunity, right, if in fact you had done it, that you could tell and explain to us? And do you get the feeling like I would understand?"

"To an extent."

"To an extent," Campion said. "Not in the sense that I've done that but to an extent, I could understand someone who had done it, 'cause I can to an extent, as much as anybody else can who can't, who hasn't done it themselves. So do you feel like as much as the cops that want to help versus the cops who just want to hammer on you, that we could understand?"

"To an extent, yeah."

"You keep saying that now. What's to an extent?"

"You can never completely understand another person, only they do. Well, even they don't sometimes."

"Right, true enough," Campion said. "I'm willing to try to understand, as much as I can, and to make other people understand as much as they can to what the real truth is. Okay?"

"Okay."

"That's where we are at."

"Then you need to find whoever did it and ask them why."

"Kind of sounds like O.J. Simpson, Dan," Campion said. "You were too young for that one."

"No, I know what you mean, but if somebody says, spreads a rumor?"

"No, it's not a rumor, because it's got fact in it. It's not making stuff up."

"Yeah, but it's fact but it's not directly correlated to me," Marsh said. "Somebody gives you facts about a crime and then points their finger at me. This is what happened, 'he did it.' That doesn't mean that I did it. Somebody within this big circle of people I'm involved with, must have done this."

"Okay," Campion said. "Why don't you talk to detective Pineda about that that big circle is and who's in that big circle. Okay?"

"Okay."

"Will you do that for me? I'm just going to go outside for a second."

"Okay."

"All right? Do you want anything?"

"Um, no. I'm fine."

"All right. I'll be right back in just a few. Ariel, this is a brand new police department, right?"

"That is correct."

The FBI man left. Pineda turned to Marsh.

Chapter 7

"Why would you fuck me over like this?"

"So what are we talking about then?"
"The circle of people."
"The string? Yeah."
"Like I told, Josh, Kevin, Sally, Alvaro, um Shandy."
"How do you spell that?"
"S-H-A-N-D-Y, Brian, Misty, Abby, Ryan, Rachel."
"And this circle of friends," Pineda said.
"I'm just trying to think of all the people that I'm even somewhat involved with."
"How do, who's the closest to you, or even in the recent past? I know you said there's been some tension."
"Alvaro tended to been closer to me than anyone."
"Who else?" Pineda said. "You said you dated? Who is it?"
"Sally."
Pineda repeated the name as he wrote.
"Brian."
"Brian's close?"
"Yeah, and Kevin," Marsh said.
"Josh's last name?"
"O'Guinn. O'Guinn. Like O-G, yeah."
"Kevin?"
"Green."
"Um, Alvaro?"
"Garibay."
"Shandy?"

"Ludwig. L, yeah."
"Brian?"
"Harty, with a T."
"Misty?
"Aguilera."
"Abby?"
"Whitcomb."
"Whitcomb?"
"Yeah."
"Like comb?" said Pineda. "Ryan?"
"Kennedy."
"And Rachel?"
"DiMarco."
"How long have you known Kevin again?"
"A year."
"How old is he?"
"Nineteen."
"And you said he's a good friend?"
"Mm-hm."
"Sally is, how long have you known her?"
"Um, about the same time, a year."
"How old is she?"
"Uh, 15."
"Alvaro?"
"I've known him four years."
"He is I think in his. . ."
"Seventeen."
"Brian's?"
"Nineteen."
"Nineteen," Pineda said. "How long have you known him?"
"Uh, two years."
"You didn't mention much when I came back in about Brian or Kevin or Sally. I think you were talking about Alvaro when you were talking to Mr. Campion here."
"He's the only one that. . ."
"You guys are really close."
"Yeah," Marsh said. "We were."

"You told each other everything?"

"Not everything, but we were pretty open."

"What about the others? Are you close with them?"

"Yeah."

The room fell silent as Pineda waited, eyes trained on Marsh.

"Like we said," the detective continued, "we're talking to everyone and we're searching everything. And the information's coming back that specifics of the information is coming from you, that you are it. And Mr. Campion is again, brought forward to you and we are, myself, and like earlier on when I was speaking to you, asking to be, try and be honest, truthful."

"I can't tell you something that I didn't do. I know that you guys want me to be the one who did this. It'd be so easy. It'd make perfect sense. It all lined up. It's fucked up but it all lined up but it isn't me. I can't confess to something I didn't do. I can't tell you why I did something if I didn't do it."

"I heard you say that already."

"I, I don't know what else you want me to say," Marsh said. "I'm being honest with you."

"So when and if at this point talking to every one of these people, they're going to say the same thing. That's what you're saying?"

"That it isn't me?"

"Yeah."

"They should," Marsh said. "I hope to God they do."

"Okay, and if they're not, then they're lying."

"I don't know."

"Yes, you do know," the detective said. "That's why we're asking you to explain why."

"I, you can add my mom on the list too, and my father if you like as well as my sister."

"In the circle you're talking about?"

"Yeah."

"Okay. I think I have their names on the first page, okay."

"So is the only evidence these facts that people have brought up?"

As he pondered the question, Pineda remained motionless.

"I don't understand. You had a question?"

"Yeah, I just. . ."

"I didn't understand it, sorry."

"So the reason you guys think it's me is because someone came in with facts?"

"Mm-hm."

"And said it was me."

"Mm-hm."

"That's kind of a far leap, when the only evidence is somebody's word against somebody else's."

"I don't know," Pineda said. "What you told me earlier shows it proves otherwise."

"Like what?"

"Tell me."

"What do you want me to tell you?"

"Tell me about Josh."

"What do you want to know?"

"Is he your close friend?"

"Somewhat close, yeah," Marsh said. "Well, he plays bass, same grade as I am, funny guy, get along well. Met him through music."

"What would he know about the homicide?"

"I don't know."

"Have you talked to him about it?"

"No. I have not really talked to anyone about it. It's, there's no point."

"What do you mean there's no point?"

"Well, like everything that happened there's no point in like, I don't know. I don't see a point in talking to all the people about the same exact thing when it's not really relevant to any of our lives. I don't like gossip and I don't like, well, social interaction in general."

"So you say you haven't talked to Josh about it?" Pineda said. "If at all, he's coming to talk to us, wouldn't have any information about it and say that he's never talked to you about it and you've never talked to him about it?"

"If we have talked about it, it was only in passing, like to hear about what happened, yeah. Nothing other than small talk about it."

"What about Kevin?"

"He would say the same thing."

"Is that where you were today?"

"Yeah."

"Last night?"

"Yeah."

"What about Sally?"

"She should say the same thing."

"What should she say?" Pineda said. "What would she say?"

"I don't know. Depends on what you ask her."

"I'm asking her the same thing as I asked about Josh and Kevin."

"Again, the only time, kind of thing we talked about, related to it is small talk in passing, talking about something that happened and we saw on the news, like anyone would. You hear about it, you talk about it."

"What would she say you told her and what would you say she say she told you? Same thing, same question I asked you about Josh, same question I asked you about Kevin."

"Yeah but I, they're not, I'm telling you, they'd just say they that we like discussed it and for like 20 seconds say, 'did you hear about that?' Oh, yeah, just quick small talk and then move on from that topic."

"Alvaro?" Pineda said. "Tell me about him?"

"I have no idea what he'd say," Pineda said. "This is the guy who over the past few weeks has consistently been trying to fuck my life up. I don't know what he's gonna say. I just hope that he's not being, he's not gonna be a dick, he's not gonna point the finger at me."

"Why would he do that?"

"I don't know why he's doing any of the things he's doing."

"Like what? I don't know what you are talking about."

"I told you about it."

"About when you were talking with Mr. Campion?"

"He reported me to the office that I had a knife, 'cause he wanted to get me out of the school," Marsh said. "He wrote a fake statement saying that I threatened him and I threatened my girlfriend, so already it's obvious that he's trying to screw me over. And I seen him by accident in passing and talk to him and I ask, 'Why did you do this to me? Why would you fuck me over like this? I never did anything to you?' And he said, 'I don't like you. I don't want to be your friend anymore. I want nothing to do with you. I don't want you here.' And then me and my girlfriend break up, and obviously he's gonna go running. . . I don't know what the hell he's trying to accomplish with all this. I don't know why he's trying to, I don't know why he's doing this."

"You say he's a close friend," Pineda said. "You should know."

"I don't. Just 'cause we're close doesn't mean like how could I know why he'd do this to me? I never did anything to him. I never hurt him. I never threatened him. All I've done is be there for him and try and help him through whatever he's going through. Is it all right if I check my phone?"

Pineda proceeded with questions.

"I have to ask about Brian. Reason why I ask is you said you were pretty close to him."

"Yeah, same thing as Josh and Kevin. Talked about it, small talk, nothing significant. Well, when something like this happens, a big, out of the ordinary holy crap event, people are gonna talk about it, people are gonna talk to their friends about it, the way people are."

"So did you talk to him about it?"

"Yeah."

"You said it was insignificant the first time."

"What?"

"You said why would you talk about this if it's insignificant to you? That's what you told me."

"It is insignificant," Marsh said. "That's why you acknowledge it and drop it."

"And you're saying these close friends of yours would say the same thing? You're telling me, you just talk about it in passing? It's nothing more?"

"Yeah," Marsh said. "Everyone except Alvaro, 'cause I don't know what the hell got into him lately."

"What about Alvaro? You haven't said anything other than what got into him but what would he say?"

"I don't know. I'm not him."

"What would these others say?"

"I just told you. It was small talk in passing."

"What did you tell them?"

"I didn't tell them anything," Marsh said. "I talked to them about it."

"Dan, I'm trying to help you."

"How?" Marsh said, jacking up his volume. "You guys are trying to pin a crime on me that I didn't commit. It's not helpful. Everything that's happened to me lately, everything in my life, I don't need this. This isn't helpful."

"Well, we may have to talk to these people," Pineda said. "I think some of them are being talked to already. I want to make sure our facts that we've received and the truth is coming out."

"Well, ask Josh, ask Kevin, ask Abby, ask my mom, ask my dad, ask my sister, ask Shandy, ask Brian. The only person I can think of who would try and screw me over is Alvaro because of the weird things he has been doing. Even that, I sure as hell hope not, because I haven't done anything to him. I haven't done anything to deserve this kind of shit."

"Who do you think I should talk to first, if they're not here already?"

"Maybe with Kevin."

"Why?"

"Cause he's my best friend and he knows me really well. The other name you got on there is David Alcalay."

"Last name?"

"Alcalay. A-L-C-A-L-A-Y. Also David Guerrero, the generic spelling."

"Who's that?"

"It's someone from school who's been helping me through a lot this year."

"Student?"

"It's my social worker."

"And David Alcalay?"

"He's just a student," Marsh said. "He's my friend."

"You mentioned all these names first, and the only one you've popped out is Kevin and these two new ones. This is your circle? I don't understand. Was this a circle of close friends?"

"It's actually a circle of people."

"You mentioned lately, and you had mentioned them in regards to, I don't understand."

"These are the people that I interact with," Marsh said. "Not all of them are close friends, but they're the people I interact with."

"Okay, I understand. Did you date any of the females here?"

"Just Sally."

"I kind of missed that. Tell me more of your relationship with Garibay?"

"With Garibay?"

"Yeah."

"What else do you want to know?"

"I mean, what you, you were in a discussion about them when I walked in," the detective said. "What, what about him in your relationship. I mean, you were saying he was close and then all of a sudden, like a brother, then all of a sudden like. . ."

"Yeah, he just all of a sudden backstabbed me," Marsh said. "I don't know why."

"Was that reason, what, your interpretation? He's not here to answer that. I'm asking you."

"I can't answer that question. I don't know why he did it."

"Oh, so you're saying you don't know but he did something. He did backstab you for something you don't know."

"He backstabbed me and I don't know why," Marsh said. "I didn't do anything to him. I did nothing. That's why this is so out of nowhere and this is why it's so painful, because people I've never done anything negative towards, they're turning against me, they're leaving me. I don't get it."

"They may give an answer to why, though?"

"Why what?"

"They're leaving you?"

"I don't know why."

"I was saying, they, they may give him, give me a reason why?"

"I don't really know. He just said he doesn't like me and he doesn't want anything to do with me."

"That's what he told you?"

"Yeah."

"And he didn't give you an explanation why?"

"No, and he said he doesn't like me anymore, he doesn't want to be my friend anymore, he wants nothing to do with me. He doesn't want me here."

"How long ago was that?"

"It was in the past couple weeks."

"What happened in the past couple weeks?"

"Nothing to prompt this," Marsh said. "That's what I'm saying, nothing even prompted any of this. That's why this makes no sense. That's why it's even that much worse because I didn't do anything."

"How long did you date Sally?"

"Six months."

"When did you guys break up?"

"The fifth of this month."

"So that's a couple of weeks," Pineda said. "Does that have anything to do with Alvaro?"

"I don't know."

"Who broke it up?"

"She did."

"What's their relationship?"

"They're best friends who started messing around lately."

"What do you mean?"

"I mean, they're best friends and they've been making out and getting physical. They haven't had sex yet, according to her, but that could be bullshit."

"Do you, is there, just asking, is there anything happened while you guys were dating, between anyone else and Alvaro?"

"What do you mean?"

"You said that they were messing around."

"Not while they were dating."

"Were they messing around while you were dating?"

"No."

"Okay," Pineda said. "Just asking."

"Yeah, I know. Just, no, she didn't."

"I mean it's uh, a breakup here in the last two weeks, and last two weeks ago, couple of weeks ago, you have a breakup with Garibay also."

"Yeah, I know," Marsh said. "It's pretty shitty."

An officer told Pineda he had a phone call. The detective did not leave the room.

"Okay. All right. Do you need any more water? Are you good there?"

"I'm all right."

"Okay, I'm gonna finish mine. Be right back." He started to leave but checked himself.

"Hey, um, Dan," the detective said. "During the investigation, uh, do you have anything on you?"

"What do you mean?"

"Do you have anything on your person, like any knives?"

"No."

"Anything like that with. . . Could you put all your stuff down here for a second?"

"Okay."

"I just want to make sure you're patted down real quick. Just turn around."

"Do you?"

"Just turn around a second."

The detective moved near Marsh.

"Yeah, just relax. . . . Nothing here?"

"Just check it," Marsh said.

"Yeah, just relax. . . Nothing here?"

"Uh, gum, money, a lighter and Chapstick."

"Okay, I'm gonna pull that out okay?"

"Okay. Um, I can do this."

"Is that a lighter?"

"No, I've got gum. I've got this like, it's like a lint roller but it's hard to explain. I can pull it out."

"Yeah. Pull it out."

"It's like you fold it open," Marsh said. "Comb, that's it for that pocket. Some money, Chapstick, house key, guitar picks."

"All right."

"And key to my room, and that's it."

"Key to your room at your mom's house?"

"Yeah, well it used to be," Marsh said. "I lost, I got my door replaced, and so now that we have locks, I have a key to my room."

"Uh, the other key goes, are those the keys to your mom's front door?"

"Yeah."

"Or somebody else's? Are you staying with your mom?"

"Yeah."

"And nowhere else?"

"Mm-hm."

Presently agent Campion returned.

Chapter 8

"You're ruining my life."

"Okay," Campion said. "Couple of things, the evidence, the investigation's going to progress, okay, so if we have to do certain things and that's what detective Pineda's looking at here, you know, some things that we need to check for evidence."

"Uh-huh."

"So a couple of things. We have a DNA swab kit here. Um, we'd like to take your DNA to check it against things that have been found at the crime scene, pretty much standard CSI kind of stuff. Any problems with that?"

"I guess not."

"Okay," Campion said. "I would actually ask Ariel to do that, since it'll be his chain of custody. The other thing is, Dan, if you don't mind sitting down taking off your boots. Okay?"

Daniel Marsh duly removed his boots.

"Now, if I understood Ariel from before," said Campion. "You told them that you had never known those people who were killed in their house."

"Yeah."

"That you kind of knew generally which one it was, or specifically which one it was?"

"No, I hadn't," Marsh said. "I didn't know until after the crime happened."

"Okay," Campion said. "And that, and I don't know if he specifically asked you, have you ever been inside of that house?"

"No."

"Either when they were there or when they weren't there?"

Marsh did not answer in his usual prompt manner.

"Wait," he said. "I went in once, when we first moved there."

"Okay," Campion said. "What were the circumstances of that?"

"We were just meeting neighbors," Marsh said. "It was just kind of a welcome thing, you know."

"Okay. So when you say when we first moved there?"

"Me and my dad. I was living with him at the time and he threw me out."

"So how long ago would that have been?"

"I don't know exactly, um, year and half, two years ago."

"Okay," said Campion. "I thought you said he kicked you out like a year and half ago?"

"Yeah, he did but we weren't living there long before that happened."

"Okay. So a period of not more than how many months?"

"I don't remember."

"Was it months or days or weeks?"

"Probably months."

"Okay. And so you would have gone over to their place, and what, how did that transpire? How did that happen?"

"Um, we were moving in," Marsh said. "We got invited over, kind of like you know, meet the neighbors, come on in, come down, 'I'm Bill,' you know."

"Do you remember their names?"

"No."

"Was there anybody in the, well, who was in the house when you went over there?"

"Just me and my dad and them."

"Okay, so your sister wasn't there, her boyfriend wasn't there?"

"No."

"Okay. And when you said 'them,' I just got to ask questions this way. I'm not leading you, but I have to ask, who was 'them?'"

"The people who live there."

"Could you describe them, or generally?"

"Um, thinking back on it," Marsh said. "I'm pretty sure it's the people who got murdered."

"Okay. So what did they look like?"

"Um, kind of old," the teen said. "The dude was sort of balding, had a gut. Chick was overweight and had long grayish hair, I think."

"Mm-hm."

"Don't really remember anything else. It was a long time ago."

"Do you remember names?"

"No."

"Okay," Campion said. "Well, that pretty well describes them. Did they have any dogs or anything like that?"

"Not that I remember."

"And where were you inside of their place?"

"They showed us around. I went in the kitchen, in the living room, showed me they, showed me their bedroom, showed me. I used their bathroom at one point, I think. I don't know. It was a long time ago."

"Now, there's two bathrooms in there," Campion said. "Do you remember which one you used?"

"I think, no. I didn't know there were two bathrooms."

"All right. The time frame again."

"A couple of years."

"A couple of years. All right. So you would have been in there with your dad, no other time, though?"

"Not that I'm aware of. It if happened, I don't remember so I highly doubt it happened."

"Okay. Just to make sure we're talking about the same place, your place was kind of a detached place, right, whereas going down a few, there's a long string of several units kind of together?"

"Yeah."

"Okay," Campion said. "Do you remember anything about the positioning of their place?"

"I don't remember if they were like one house over or two houses over."

"Okay. Were they a single, was your place with your dad a single family house, like, uh, or was it a duplex?"

"Just a single house thing."

"Okay. So you don't share a wall with anybody else?"

"No."

"Okay."

"I don't think so. If it's a duplex, then it's a massive duplex."

"All right, and then, but the place that these older folks live in, that is a connection of several places. I don't know if you realized that, but do you remember the color of the house or any details about it?"

"Um, the same color as my dad's, I think. Green? I'm color blinded, I'm sorry."

"For real?"

"Yeah."

"Wow," Campion said. "Okay, so, but two years ago, a year and a half to two years ago, you might have been in there and you might have walked around and they might have showed you the place."

"Yeah."

"How many bedrooms do you remember?"

"One."

"Do you remember anything particular about the place that, was there any specific thing that struck you about the inside of their, their place?"

"Yeah," Marsh said. "They had a lot of mirrors."

"A lot of mirrors?"

"Yeah."

"What's that all about?"

"I don't know."

"It's interesting."

"Didn't really feel like asking."

"Did you have a theory at the time, or no?"

"No, I was, I wasn't really interested in it. I guess, just a bunch of mirrors."

"Okay. Um, how long have you had these boots?"

"Uh, since the eighth grade."

"Since the eight grade? Your feet haven't grown since the eighth grade?"

"No, they got to damn near size 10 and then they just . . ."

"Okay. Anything, unusual about these?"

"I don't, I don't, I don't think so."

"Have you ever worn them around blood?"

"Um, maybe," Marsh said. "I get a lot of nose bleeds."

"So?"

"Maybe they got on that."

"Okay, but if that was to be the case, it would be your blood?"

"I assume," Marsh said.

"Um, any other places you've walked through, like major bloody things, like deer getting hit in the road and you walk through, anything like that?"

"Might have walked through like road kill, like, I don't know," Marsh said. "After years of having 'em, I don't' really think a lot about what I'm walking on."

"Okay."

"Yes, definitely possible."

"Is there any reason that you would ever put duct tape on the bottom of those boots, Dan?"

"No."

"No?"

"I put some in here," Marsh said. "That's 'cause that was rubbing against my ankle."

"So some duct tape inside the, the uppers here."

"Yeah."

"By where the green skeleton is? How about this one?"

"No. It was only that one that had the problem."

"Okay, but never on the bottom?"

"No."

"Okay," said Campion. "So there's no, there would be no reason for there to be duct tape residue on the bottom of your boots?"

"No, there shouldn't be."

"Have you ever lent your boots out to anybody?"

"No."

"Are they what you wear most every day?"

"Yeah."

"Do you have another pair of shoes?"

"No."

"These are it, then," Campion said. "These are the only pair of shoes that you have?"

"They're the only pair I wear. I have these Converse, but I haven't worn them in a long time."

"Okay. And where would those be?"

"Uh, I think I got rid of them, or they're somewhere in my house. No, I got rid of them."

"Okay. So these are it. These are what you wear?"

"Yeah."

"Go back from, say, this year, 2013. Are these the only pair of shoes that you've had, or have you ever had another pair of shoes that you would have bought, maybe didn't like, and threw away?"

"Just these."

"Any other clothing that you bought and didn't like and threw away in 2013?"

"Not that I remember."

"Okay. Do you usually wear a jacket during the winter?"

"Uh, sometimes."

"What kind of jacket?"

"Um, usually a windbreaker, or like a denim jacket. I have one of those."

"Like a blue jean denim jacket, or is it black?"

"It's blue."

"Okay, or a windbreaker? What color is the windbreaker?"

"Uh, I think it's red. I don't know what the . . ."

"Oh, that's right," Campion said. "You're colorblind."

"Yeah. It's kind of . . ."

"What's your problem you, like what? The ones in the corner there, what color are those? What color is that package?"

"Yellow."

"And what color is your lighter?"

"Red."

"Red all over or?"

"Do you mean the lighter or the lighter case?"

"Uh, sorry, the lighter case."

"Um, that's pink, and that's darker red."

"Okay. All right. Um, so any jackets that you've thrown away though, or any other clothing that you for whatever reason would have thrown away?"

"I don't think so," Marsh said.

"This year, in 2013, say?"

"No."

"Nasty Christmas present you didn't like?"
"No, I really don't think I threw anything away."
"Okay. Got rid of, gave to anybody else?"
"I don't remember," Marsh said, "And nothing comes to mind."
"Okay. All right."
Pineda opened his buccal swab kit.
"I just want to have five seconds each," the detective said. "I'll just go ahead and wipe this down here by your cheek and then this one here off your left. Okay. Just open up? And, your left. Okay, open up."
When the detective finished, Marsh said, "So like can I go home? I haven't eaten all day?"
"Uh, we have some pizza here," Pineda said. "I think we offered you some pizza."
"Uh, I'm kind of a health nut."
"Oh, so what kind of stuff you eat?"
"Uh, I don't know, mainly base my stuff on low-fat diet."
"On which fat?"
"Low fat."
"Oh, low fat," Pineda said. "I though you said yolo fat. I'm like, what's yolo? Those are for you if you're hungry."
"Well it's more like uh, it's been a pretty stressful day," Marsh said, "I'm kind of."
"Kind of what, Dan?" Campion said.
"Just kind of want to go home."
"So," Campion continued, "another piece of evidence that we want to follow up on is this phone. Is this the phone? How long have you had this phone?"
"Uh, a long time. Uh, like a year."
"A year? So going back into 2012 for sure? No ifs ands or buts. And you keep that phone pretty much all the time with you?"
"Um, usually, yeah."
"I mean, most people do, certainly most teenagers."
"Sometimes I forget, but . . ."
"But you don't have to," Campion said. "Or you don't give it to anybody else or, you know, to use?"
"Well, I let people use it when they need to make calls, and that's about it."

"Okay. But as far as taking away, your sister doesn't borrow it from you, or your girlfriend?"

"Um, no."

"Seeing you, you wouldn't take it away and say 'I need your phone?' Nothing like that? Okay."

"What's the phone number on this?" asked Pineda.

"It's the one I gave you."

"Oh, okay," Campion responded, repeating the number. "So that phone is certainly, as you know, Dan, a piece of almost tracking equipment, if you will, in today's day and age. Cause if anything, the NSA or the FBI or anything like that's been in the news recently, but just because that's what phones are. Whenever you walk around, you hit different cell phone towers and it pretty much gives an imprint. We can go back and locate where that phone was a particular day and a particular time."

"Yes, I know."

"Did you know that?"

"Yes."

"Okay, so where is your phone going to show you were the night that these two people were killed?"

"A friend's house."

"A friend's house," Campion said. "You told me, possibly Kevin's? Where does Kevin live?"

"Uh, I don't remember the address," Marsh said. "I just know his house by the look of it. It's where, also where he picked me up from."

"All right," detective Pineda said. "So I thought you told me you were at Kevin's today. That's where he picked you up?"

"Yeah."

"Okay so that, whatever that address is, and I don't know Davis geography that well. Where is that in relation to here?"

"Um, not that far, like by Dollar Tree kind of."

"On Eighth Street," Pineda said.

"This side of the freeway or the other side of the freeway?"

"This side," Pineda said. "Just north of us."

"Can I go home?" said Marsh.

"Close to Pole Line," Pineda said, a reference to Pole Line Road, a north-south artery in Davis.

"Look," Campion said. "Let's just finish my thought on the phone here. If that phone is gonna be showing where you were and it shows that during that time where those people might have been killed that you were at your mom's house, then that's a pretty good piece of evidence, right?"

"Yeah."

"If it's showing that you were on the other side of the freeway, not such a good piece of evidence for you? Correct?"

"Yeah."

"Because it would show you lied to Ariel about where you were."

"Okay."

"And to me, because you said that you don't go to your dad's house, he kicked you out, you hadn't been there, and certainly during the time period where these people were killed, you're saying you were with your mom or with Kevin."

"Yeah."

"On this side of the freeway?"

"Yes."

"Okay."

"Can I please go?" Marsh said. "I've been here all day."

"So we'd like to take your phone."

"I kinda need that to, you know, communicate with my mother and friends."

"Well, um, as with your shoes, Dan, this part's all taken as evidence, because a judge has signed a search warrant for it."

"How am I supposed to call people or walk without my shoes?"

"Well," Campion said. "I don't think you're gonna have to worry about that, Dan."

"Am I under arrest?"

"Ariel, do you want to talk to him about that?"

"Yes or no?" Marsh said. "Am I under arrest?"

"Is there anything else you have to say to us?" said detective Pineda.

"I want to go home. I've been here all day. This has been incredibly stressful. Am I under arrest 'cause someone pointed the finger at me?"

"Yeah," Campion said, "and they said you had specific information."

"Yeah, they told you specific information and blamed me and I'm the one in trouble."

"Mm-hm," agreed Campion.

"Because that makes total sense, doesn't it?"

"It does, actually," said Campion. "So the investigation goes where it goes, Dan."

"Can't I go home until then since there's no actual evidence saying I did something?"

"Well, that's going to be up to the judge and the district attorney and all that kind of good stuff."

"Then where am I going?"

"You're going to be, you're a juvenile," Pineda said. "You'll be placed in custody at cell probation."

"Where's that?"

"Yolo Juvenile Hall here in Yolo County, Woodland."

"Why? There's, there's nothing saying I did anything. Why am I going to jail?"

"As we have spoken to you here," Pineda said, "the facts and information in regard to the homicides, to place you under arrest for that. That's why you are under arrest."

"What about the people who've told you all this extra facts, all this information? The people who've actually told you the details? What about them?"

Pineda and Campion offered no response.

"It's okay, keep ignoring me," Marsh said. "That's cool."

As another officer offered to explain how they could play back a telephone call, Marsh continued his monologue.

"So me, who has said absolutely nothing, that no person who was there would know, is under arrest but the people who have been telling you information, nothing, nothing? Just me? Not the people who've given you all this explicit information that only the people would know? The people who . . ."

"Okay. So it's not just people, Dan," Campion said. "I mean, we're not making this stuff up. Okay?"

"Well, what do you mean it's not people?"

"So there's a recording that we have."

"Of what?"

"Of a phone call. I want you to hear and listen to it."

Pineda started the recording. Marsh heard the voice of his friend Alvaro.

"Like I guess you went to a concert and . . . so yeah."

The next voice was Sally's.

"Hello?"

"Hey," said Alvaro. "Um I'm at like the police station and like I've been talking to them a lot."

"Yeah?"

"They like want to know a lot about Daniel and they want to know if you can talk about it."

"Me?"

"Yeah."

"Uh, the stabbing thing."

"Yeah," Alvaro said. "I mean, like the double homicide."

"Yeah."

"Uh, there's a detective like if you want to get picked up. She's really cool. She's uh, detective KB and she's like really cool hair and I've been talking to her a lot."

"Yeah?"

"Yeah, and like yeah you feel a lot better, cause actually I feel a lot better about it, 'cause you know?"

"Oh," she said. "Wait, they're gonna pick me up."

"Yeah, uh, well do you want to get picked up, or like can you?"

"Uh."

"Or would that be okay?"

"I don't, like I don't know if I can."

"Like do you, are you busy today?"

"Uh, like hella family's over at my house right now."

"Okay. Well, I mean," Alvaro's voice said. "Well, like it would be really cool if you could like do that."

Marsh said, "Uh, that's from Sally right?"

"Is that who you think it is?" Campion said.

"It's who it sounds like," Marsh said.

"Okay."

The voice continued, "Are there any other options, like where I can talk to her?"

"I mean, I know their voices," Marsh said. "Sounds like them."

"Well, I don't know," Alvaro said. "I feel like it'd be better if you just came over here, well can you talk to the Davis police department?"

"Would I go on my own?"

"I think so. Uh, well, she doesn't, like she can talk to you there."

"Uh, she can she can come over here, like she doesn't have to take me anywhere?"

"Yeah."

"That might be better' cause if I leave," she said, "my mom might like, my whole family's just gonna be like, okay, what's going on, and it'll be like, yeah, it's gonna be a whole big mess."

"Yeah. All right, well . . ."

"That works."

"Do you think you can like . . ."

"I'm doing okay. How are you?"

"I'm really good, actually," Alvaro said. "Like it's really fun actually. It's really fun actually, like it's that. . ."

After an inaudible response, Alvaro continued.

"Um, yeah, okay. So listen, I apologize about the clip. She says she'll be there in 30 minutes."

"Okay. All right, hold on. I'll be on . . ."

"Alright."

"All right, do you want to like, yeah."

"Uh, yeah, I'll, I can talk to you later. Yeah."

"Um, no . . ."

On that note, the recorded call ended. Marsh sat in silence.

"So, I mean," Campion said, "you can tell that there's recordings and stuff like that, and tell me about the time, you said the last time you talked to her was a few days ago. Tell me about how that happened? How did you go to her? How'd you meet with her?"

"Uh, I went to the house in Dixon and I talked with her."

"How did you?" Campion said. "Did you knock on the front door?"

"No."

"And wait for her parents to answer?"

"No."

"How did you do that?"

"She came outside and we talked."

"Really?"

"Yeah," Marsh said. "She well, she came outside and then brought me in and we went into her room and talked."

"How, how did you get into the room, or to the house?"

"I went through the back."

"Through the door?"

"So went in through the back door?"

"Yes."

"Okay. So?"

"Can I ask something?" Marsh said.

"Well, I'm gonna ask you why you are lying about that," Campion said. "Or why would she tell us a completely different story about how this last contact went, Dan?"

"Well, I went there and I went in."

"Yeah."

"And I talked to her."

"That's completely different than what you just said. How did you go in? Tell the truth."

"I went through the back door."

"Through what part of the back door?"

"The doggy door."

"The doggy door, okay," Campion said. "So this is the whole thing about it all right. You're gonna play hard to get. You're gonna try to lie. You're gonna try to shade, you're gonna try to leave out things that are inconvenient for you, and that's not consistent with someone who's saying, 'I didn't do this.' Okay? It makes no sense."

"I'm fucking scared."

"Then tell me."

"I'm so terrified."

"Then tell the truth," Campion said. "Don't lie. You went through the doggy door."

"This is my life."

"Late at night, and you went in and surprised her. She had no idea you were coming, and you're there, poof, suddenly."

"It was a romantic gesture."

"Is that what happened?"

"Yes," Marsh said. "It was a romantic gesture. I always used to say, 'you know, one of these days I'm just gonna show up and surprise you.'"

"So if it was a romantic gesture, Dan, then why the heck would you just sit here and bald-face lie to Ariel and me?"

"Cause I am . . . you guys are threatening me with fucking . . ."

"With what?" Campion said. "The truth?"

"Including lying to the police, two police officers who have been sitting here talking to you for. . ."

"Don't be a dick, okay?" Marsh said. "Don't just take like a tone all of a sudden. You were being hella friendly and now all of a sudden. . ."

"You lied to me, Dan, and I know you lied about that."

"You're, you're ruining my life. Why should I . . ."

"I'm not ruining your life," Campion said. "I'm trying to solve a homicide, a double homicide, and if you do it, I understand. And I am there for you to try, to make other people understand, 'cause I see it. I see it in you. And you're not alone. You're not the only one. I know it feels like you're the only one, but you're not."

"If you want to help me, then don't ruin my life," Marsh said. "If anything, send me to the psychiatric hospital."

"Okay," Campion said. "We can talk about that."

"I'd rather go there than jail."

"Okay."

"I mean, I'm psychotic, that has some, that has to . . ."

"You told me earlier you that weren't psychotic."

"Did I?"

"Yeah."

"Are you sure?"

"I am," Campion said.

"I don't remember saying that."

"You did. I asked you if you had taken the . . ."

"No, you asked me if the medication wasn't anti-psychotic, not if I was psychotic. You asked me about the medication, and it technically is an addition to an anti-depression to stabilize mood."

"It is, so I asked you if you ever had any psychotic episodes or psychosis indicators and you said no. I remember it. So don't lie to me, okay? We're pretty good at what we do. All right. And I'm not trying to ruin your life."

"Well, you're doing a good job then."

"I'm not trying to ruin your life. I'm trying to help you get through this difficult time and if the psychiatric hospital is where you should go, then the first step down that road, Dan, is right now, right today."

"I'd rather be in a psychiatric hospital than in jail."

"Okay," Campion said. "Then tell us what happened and why. That's what I'm saying. I don't doubt that you may end up down there, that road, and exactly in that place, and get help there and get treatment."

"Until it's proven, unless you can prove with the actual evidence, that it was me, then I'm not gonna. . ."

"So if I show you proof that it was actually you, if I have physical evidence that it was you, you're not going to admit anything?"

"No, if you . . ."

"You're gonna continue to lie to me? That's what you're saying?"

"No, what I'm saying is, unless you can show me something that flat out says it was you, then why would I say, okay, it was me?"

"If you think you belong in a psychiatric hospital, then that's because you have all this stuff in your house, you have all this stuff in your brain, you just want to be outside of your head but you can't. This is the only thing that gave you a place, a safe place, a place to land, a refuge, anything that gets you to feel."

"I'm fucked either way, aren't I?"

"Pretty much," Campion said. "Pretty much. Just tell us that you need help."

"I need help," Marsh said.

"Okay. That's the first step."

Campion paused and gathered his thoughts.

"So let's go back to the first time you thought about killing someone," he said. "How long ago was that?"

They were loving people, peaceful people, spiritual people.

Chip Northup, far left, liked that "old timey" folk music

Scene of the double murder. The killer once lived only steps away.

Out front the warning sign held vigil, to no avail.

"My name's Dan and I like the dark," said Marsh, third row, center.

The defendant drew support around Davis.

Chip Northup practiced law in the same Yolo County Courthouse where his killer was tried.

All photos by Lloyd Billingsley.

Chapter 9

"It felt great. Like it was pure happiness."

"Years ago," Marsh said.

"How many years?"

"Six."

"Six," Campion said. "So when you were like 10?"

"When I was 10 I thought about and plotted about killing a woman that my mother left my father for."

"Your kindergarten teacher?"

"Yes."

"Because you were so angry at her?"

"Yeah."

"Okay."

"I saw her as the reason that my family was ripped apart and in a way she was a big part of that."

"So she was gonna be held responsible? Okay, so what? What were you gonna do at age 10? What was your plan?"

"I was going to slit her throat."

"Okay, how were you going to do that?"

"I knew where she lived," Marsh said. "She came over frequently. I didn't at the time really, I was 10 I didn't have a plan."

"Okay. Did you ever take any steps towards that one? Did you go over to her house and try to get in at night?"

"No."

"Or at least watch what her habits were or, did you have a knife at the time?"

"Well, I had access to knives but I didn't have one that I can call my own."

"Okay," Campion said. "So when's the next time that you remember thinking about killing someone, Dan?"

"Uh, about seventh grade."

"And who was that?"

"It wasn't anyone in particular. It was just I thought about, everybody at that school gave me so much shit that I just thought about just showing up one day and seeing how many I could take out before they took me out."

"The anger was boiling over."

"Yeah."

"Did you ever? How far did you get in that one? Did you ever try to find a gun?"

"Yeah, I tried but I didn't really succeed."

"Does your family have guns?"

"No."

"Your dad doesn't have any? When was the next time you remember thinking about killing someone?"

"Eighth grade, I still had the same desire."

"School," Campion said. "So this is middle school now?"

"Yeah. Ninth grade is when it got more intense, more every time I look at someone in my mind, in my mind I see flashes of images of me killing them."

"Okay."

"In numerous ways," Marsh said, "In numerous horrible ways, doing terrible things. I can't help it. It's just what comes into my head when I see them. I don't want it to. I don't like it that it does, but it does."

"Right."

"And that's around the time all that started."

"There were other people at school or students?"

"It's with everyone," Marsh said.

"Everyone?"

"Everyone I look at."

"Okay. Family members?"

"Family members, most of them, doesn't matter," Marsh said. "Fucking disgusting, but it's what it is."

"Okay, well."

"It's not a desire, it's a thought."

"It just appears."

"Yeah. I don't enjoy it."

"Okay. When was the first time you started thinking about killing these people down the street?"

"Yeah, I really am fucked either way, aren't I?" Marsh said. "I didn't. . ."

"Did you start thinking about it?"

"I, that night I just, I couldn't take it anymore. I had to do it. I lost control."

"Okay."

"I just went into the street and wandered around for a while. I just, looking for who would be, which house I should go to, who would be a good victim."

"Okay. Were you by yourself, Dan?"

"Yes."

"What time of night was it?"

"It was like two in the morning, two or three."

"Okay," Campion said. "Do you remember what day of the week it was?"

"I think it was a Friday night, either Friday night or Saturday night."

"Okay. And when you say you went out in the street, where did you start out that evening, that night?"

"Um, well, I just kind of walked all around south Davis."

"Okay. So, and where do you remember next? Where do you, how do you find yourself over by your dad's house?"

"Well, I'd been walking down the streets trying, scoping out apartment complexes and houses, just trying to see, uh, who would be, which one can I do it to, who left their door unlocked, whose window is open."

"Okay."

"And uh, everyone had done a good job of locking their doors and closing their windows until I got to that house."

"All right," Campion said. "So what did you do then?"

"I went around the back," Marsh said. "Just for clarification, you're telling me that whether I tell you what I'm about to tell you or not, that I'm gonna be, I'm gonna, it's done."

Campion and Pineda did not respond.

"Okay," Marsh continued. "I cut a hole in the screen, not even a hole, just a flap that I could get in and out with, climbed in through the back, listened for snoring. I heard it, went to their bedroom. I opened the door, then I just kind of stood over their bed, watching them sleep for a few minutes. My body was trembling. I was nervous but excited and exhilarated. I was actually gonna do it. I was there. It was finally happening. It was almost like an out of body experience. I just, I didn't feel like I was there, like it was real. And the woman woke up, so I just started stabbing, over and over."

"Okay."

"In the torso and I tried to get. . . and then the husband woke up and he looked over, and just as he looked over, I stabbed him in the neck. And then I went back to killing the woman, 'cause she wouldn't die."

"You're stabbing her in the torso," Campion said after a pause, "and she just wouldn't die?"

"Yeah, like I, I stabbed her a lot as you obviously know. It took a long time. I don't know, it was a lot easier with the guy than it was with her."

"Where did you stab him?"

"Well," Marsh said. "I started in the neck and then I just kind of went all over. And well, I stabbed her until she stopped moving and she was just kind of twitching, and I went over to him 'cause I'd only stabbed him once at the time, 'cause you know, I had to finish that one. And I started stabbing him in the torso as well. Um, made sure they were both dead and then I just kind of kept stabbing their dead bodies. Don't know why. It just felt right."

"Okay," Campion said. "So even after they stopped moving?"

"Even when they were dead, I wasn't done," Marsh said. "And I just kind of messed around with, messed around with them. I cut open both their torsos, you around here, and in the woman I put a phone inside of her and I put a cup inside the guy. I don't know why. I really don't."

"Okay."

"And then I like cut open her leg. I don't know why I did that, either. I just kind of wanted to see. It was disgusting."

"Not what you expected?"

"Yeah," Marsh said. "I never actually seen like what fat actually looks like."

"What surprised you about it?"

"I'm not really sure, like so that's what makes people fat. There's just like this material, like this substance. It smelled bad."

"A lot of people don't recognize, don't recognize that that's what happens. It does smell bad. What color was it? Do you remember?"

"It was yellow."

"Okay."

"Um, I kind of like pulled some of it out with the knife 'cause I was interested and I wanted to see what else was inside."

"We still talking about that leg on the women now or are we talking about the torso?"

"Um, it was the torso that I pulled more of it out of. I don't remember if I pulled some out of the leg or not."

"Okay. And so the cup and the phone, who, what did you put into whom?"

"I put the phone into the woman and the cup into the man."

"Where did you find those?"

"In the kitchen."

"Okay," Campion said. "What else did you do in the kitchen when you were, what led you into the kitchen to see the cup and the phone?"

"The kitchen was on the way to the back where I came in from, and I was hanging out and then I was like, I don't even know. Honestly, I just wanted to fuck with the people who had to like investigate it."

"Yeah," Campion said. "That would be us."

"Yeah."

"Throw them off, make it look a little. . ."

"Make it look, just, what the hell?"

"It worked," Campion said.

"I figured. Um, that's pretty much it."

"Okay," Campion said. But Marsh wasn't done.

"Stabbed the hell out of them," he said. "I don't know how many times each. I lost count. I cut open their torsos, I cup open her leg. I think I cut open his as well. I don't really remember."

"Do you remember any other cuttings on his body in particular. Anywhere else?"

"Just like a lot in the torso and in the sides, and neck. Oh, in the forehead, cut his forehead too."

"What was that about?"

"I don't know," Marsh said. "I just wanted to like. I just wanted to. . ."

"Was it exploration, curiosity?"

"Kinda yeah," Marsh said. "Plus I never really actually stabbed somebody, so I wanted to see how effective the knife was. And I kind of like, I punched him a few times."

"At what point? At the beginning?"

"No. This was when they were dead."

"This was after they were dead?" Campion said. "Okay."

"Just kind of like, hit them a bunch."

"Both of them."

"Mainly the guy."

"Is that part of the anger coming out, the rage coming out?"

"All of it was."

"Yeah."

"I'm not gonna lie," Marsh said. "It felt amazing."

"How did it feel, Dan?"

"Just, it felt great. Like it was, it was pure happiness, and adrenaline and dopamine, just all of it, uh, rushing over me. It was the most exhilarating, enjoyable feeling I've ever felt."

"I've heard other people talk about it and it's been better than even sex. Better than sexual . . ."

"Yeah."

"Release," Campion said.

"It was."

"How long did it last?"

"Um the rest of that night and for a few days, actually. Yeah, for a while, probably a week."

"All right, but you really had a problem because you can't tell anybody. Did anybody actually comment to you about it?"

"In what way?"

"That you seem different, that you seem happy, you seemed euphoric?"

"I don't think so."

"Okay," Campion said. "But eventually you did talk to some people? Who did you talk to?"

"I talked to Sally. I talked to Alvaro. Really fucking stupid."

"So what you told them was the truth of what actually happened?"

"Yeah."

"Okay."

After a long pause, detective Pineda spoke up.

"Anyone else you told?"

"No."

"And they weren't there?" Campion said. "Nobody else was there?"

"No, it was just me."

"How long were you inside the room?" Pineda said.

"Uh, probably half an hour."

"Okay," Pineda said. Campion resumed his questions.

"Let's go back up and start from seeing them from the back, seeing that the window, or was it the sliding glass door that you saw?"

"The window was open, so I cut like kind of a flap like in the screen."

"Okay. What part of the screen got cut, so this is you know, if this thing is the window, where's the screen?"

Campion held up a tablet.

"It was over here," Marsh said, showing where he had cut the screen. "I got like, I'm pretty sure it was like that, so kind of like a doggie door."

"So the whole, if this whole thing is the screen?"

"Oh, if this whole thing is the screen?"

"Yeah."

"Um, not, it was like . . ."

"So pretty much all around the borders of the screen?"

"Yeah."

"Okay," Campion said. "What were you wearing when you went in?"

"Um, those boots, um, black socks, black pants like these, black undershirt, black jacket, uh, black gloves, and a black ski mask."

"Okay. Where are those things now?"

"In my garage."

"At your mom's house? And what are they inside of?"

"I don't know. I dispersed them all throughout the garage."

"So the black ski mask, the black gloves? What kind of gloves?"

"Um, I don't really know how to describe it," Marsh said. "They were like, I don't know how to describe it."

"What would you use those type of gloves for?"

"Um, not really any purpose, just kind of for like to keep your hands warm."

"Okay," Campion said. "Men's gloves, women's gloves?"

"Uh, I think they were women's. They went like high."

"Higher up?"

"Yeah."

"Okay. All right. And jacket, um, black jacket. Is that there too?"

"Yeah."

"Is it a windbreaker that you had talked about or the other one? Or is it separate?"

"No," Marsh said. "It's a different one."

"What does it look like?"

"It's big, bulky, uh, it's like kind of a pilot's jacket only without the collar."

"Okay. Is it black on the inside and the outside?"

"No, just the outside."

"Just the outside? And is it yours, or is it somebody else's?"

"It's mine."

"Okay. Did you wash blood off it or? It had to have been fairly covered?"

"I kept it as a souvenir," Marsh said.

"Okay. So where is the jacket, inside the garage, as close as you can remember? You said you dispersed it around."

"It's by the guitar case."

"By the guitar case?"

"Yeah."

"In your mom's garage?"

"Yeah."

"And pants, you had some pants on?"

"Yeah, well, I washed those, and I own three pairs of pants like this, so it might be these, it might be the other two, I don't know. So you're not gonna find anything on them. I already washed it and everything."

"Okay."

"All the evidence you need is in that garage."

"Okay," Campion continued. "The hat, the gloves, the jacket. And then the boots, did you do anything to clean the boots off?"

"Um, I rinsed them with a hose."

"Did they have a lot of blood on them?"

"No, not really," Marsh said. "I don't think like, I don't think they had any. I was just being careful, 'cause I mean, all the blood was on the bed."

"Okay. Uh, the ski mask, typical ski mask with holes?"

"No, It only had one hole."

"One hole?"

Marsh outlined the area around his eyes.

"There."

"Okay. All right. And how did you? Did you have that ski mask, usually not? Most people don't have a ski mask like that."

"No."

"Where did you get that from?"

"I stole it from Big Five."

"Okay," Campion said. "So, how long before?"

"Couple weeks."

"Couple weeks? And how about the jacket?"

"I had that for a long time, like a year."

"Okay. Did you get that in anticipation of doing this?"

"No."

"All right. The gloves?"

"Those are just in my house."

"Your house, your mom's or somebody's?"

"Somebody's."

"All right," said Campion. "Okay, how about the knife, Dan. Where's that?"

"It's in the garage. It should be on one of the shelves when you walk in on the left."

"And what does it look like?"

"It's a Buck knife. Have you ever seen the movie *Scream*?"
"Mm-hm."
"It's like the Ghost Face knife."
"Ghost Face knife."
"Like that exact one," Marsh said. "I thought it was kind of cool."
"Where did you get that?"
"I found it in my mom's bedroom."
"Oh, it's your mom's?"
"Yeah," Marsh said. "I found it under her desk."
"How long before?"
"A few weeks."
"Okay," Campion said. "All right, and then when you go in, said you cut out the screen, and it's in the window or door, just want to be sure?"
"The window."
"And where, where do you come into when you're first in?"
"When did I come in?"
"Where to? What part of the house do you come into?"
"The back window, where the screen was."
"Does it go into, what room?"
"The room with all the mirrors."
"The room with all the mirrors, okay. Is that when you noticed that, did that scare you? Did that shock you when you?"
"It kind of startled me 'cause I was like walking and I saw my reflection everywhere and I wasn't sure at first, you know, like 'Oh crap.'"
Marsh laughed as he described the scene.
"There's another guy in here."
"All right. And then beforehand, did you go anywhere else in the house. Like you said, you were listening for snoring, you heard it?"
"Yeah, no, I just walked through the kitchen to the door."
"You walked through, you walked through the kitchen?"
"I think so."
"And you went to the bedroom?"
"Yeah."
"Because at that point," Campion said, "I mean, you know what you're there for."
"Well, yeah, I'm already here," Marsh said. "There's no backing out now."

"Too far down the road?"

"Basically."

"It's gonna happen."

"I didn't want to back out."

"Okay."

"It isn't me," Marsh said. "I wasn't myself. I didn't even feel real."

"You didn't even feel real? Beforehand, are we talking beforehand, you didn't feel real? Or was there . . ?"

"Throughout the whole time. . ."

"Yeah."

"I didn't feel real."

"The out of body experience."

"I have dreams of things like that all the time," Marsh said. "I have dreams of me hurting and killing and doing horrible things."

"How long have those been?"

"Uh, two years, about, and then just it felt like another dream, but when I woke up next morning and it actually happened."

"Okay. When you were in there beforehand, you're listening, then you go in and she wakes up. Did you say anything to her?"

"It took her like," Marsh said. "I was in the room for a few minutes before she woke up. I was trying to figure how I was going to do it, 'cause I didn't expect, it was, you know, who do I get first, kind of thing. I didn't say anything to her when she woke up. She woke up and looked at me and gasped. And just like looking at me while I'm standing over you dressed all in black with a mask and a knife. Like there's no explanation for that."

"So had you started stabbing her when she woke up? Or did she wake up before you started stabbing her?"

"She woke up before."

"And how much time would you say before she realized you were there?"

"Two seconds."

"Two seconds," Campion said. "All right. And so you started stabbing her. Are you right-handed or left-handed?"

"I use my right hand."

"Okay."

"I actually at one point took out my phone with the left hand and shined it so I could see better."

"Okay, that was one thing I was going to ask. Did you have a flashlight then?"

"No."

"So but then you had this phone?"

"Yeah."

"That it just kind of illuminated a little bit so you could see."

"Yeah."

"What you were doing. All right. And then he woke up at some point. Did she? Was she screaming, or was she making any noise?"

"Yeah," Marsh said. "She screamed."

"Loud, medium, muffled?"

"Medium. It got muffled 'cause I put my hand on her mouth."

"Okay. All right. And then he woke up?"

"Yeah, the second he woke up he like turned over, looked and me and then I, soon as I saw him turn over, just reached over and got him right here."

Marsh held a hand to his neck.

"Like the right side of his jaw?" Campion said.

"Yeah, under his jaw."

"Did you feel it penetrated a lot? Was it, was it a good one?"

"Yeah, they all were," Marsh said. "I actually like, I felt skin and bone a few times."

"Okay. And that stopped him from resisting at that point?"

"Well, yeah, by then he was just like grabbing his neck trying to stop it and bleeding everywhere. It was like gargling and stuff."

"Was there blood spurt at all?" Campion said. "Was there blood spurting around, or could you tell?"

"I couldn't tell but I doubt it. It looked like it was just kind of draining."

"How about with her? Were you like stabbing her through like the sheets?"

"No, she um, I think she woke up to go to the bathroom or something, 'cause she woke up and threw off the sheet and that's when I was like, whoa."

"Here we go."

"Pretty much," Marsh said. "It was a lot messier than. . . It didn't go how I expected."

"What was different?"

"Well, I just, I figured like I'd sneak in and just like slit their throats and take it from there. This was a lot more exciting, more intense."

"The actual stabbing was more exciting and intense than slitting their throat?"

"Because it was actually like, they were awake and like knowing and resisting."

"So that heightened the experience?"

"Yeah."

Chapter 10

"I want to hurt people. I want to kill people."

After a brief pause, Campion continued.

"Everything you've been telling us, Dan, is very consistent with the other people I've talked to who've done this as well. I don't know if that's comforting in any way, but you're not alone in that."

"Do you think I'll get the death penalty? I don't know, that's kind of far-fetched."

"You were 15, right?"

"Yeah, I was 15, and got psychological issues up the wazoo."

"We've talked a lot about those today," Campion said. "Are there any other ones that, at the end we were talking about whether or not you said that you ever had experienced psychosis or not. If when we get, when we get the medical records and all that, is that ever, is that gonna pop up?"

"It should. They put me on anti-psychotics it seems like. I was in the hospital in Sacramento."

"Did you ever hear any voices talking to you?"

"No."

"Did you ever have any hallucinations about things that weren't there? Thinking that things were there when they really weren't?"

"Uh, I occasionally would like, I'd see something and then I'd like look again and it wouldn't be there, but I think that was just my mind messing with me or my vision. 'Cause it was never like a full-on, like I never looked at it for more than half a second."

"Okay. You ever have people talking to you and, and then they, they'd just start, you're perceiving they're saying completely random and different things? That they're, it turns out that they're really not saying? Anything like that?"

"I don't think so."

"Okay," Campion said. "How forthcoming were you with the psychiatrist and the medical people that looked at you back in December?"

"I was pretty straight with them."

"Did you talk about the dreams?"

"No."

"Okay. All right. So, getting back to the inside of the apartment, after it's all over and, did you go, when you said you were finished with her you went to him. Physically did you just reach across or?"

"No. It was over to the other side."

"Went around to the other side of the bed. Okay. Estimate how many times you might have stabbed him?"

"I'm trying to think, uh, like at least 20 times. I don't know, you guys should know the actual count, right?"

"We, we have to ask, yeah."

"I think it was like that, minimum of 20, probably no more than like 30. I don't know."

"Okay."

"I didn't count."

"How about with her?"

"Same."

"Okay," Campion said. "I think it's gonna turn out to be more, but that's neither here nor there. So, and then, how long was it then when they stop moving, and how did you come to the conclusion that they were dead?"

"Well, I mean, I kind of just took a knife blade this long and shoved it into their bodies more times than I could count."

"Right. But it's surprising that she kept on moving for as long as she did?"

"Yeah, it took her a long time," Marsh said. "It took him less time to die, but I think that's 'cause I started with his neck. But, um, they shit themselves."

"Okay."

"So that's kind of when I knew, like all right, well, they're done."

"And how did you know that?"

"Um, when you die you void your bowels," Marsh said, "and I figured it was a combination of that and from the pain."

"Okay. How did you know they had shit themselves? Pretty obvious?"

"It was pretty kind of, well the same way you know, anyone does," Marsh said with a laugh.

"You hear it, and you sure as hell smell it."

"So that, did you take their pulse? Did you do anything like that?"

"Yeah, I did, just to be sure, at the end."

"Where did you take their pulse?"

"Uh, jugular."

"Okay, for both of them? All right. And through the gloves, they were thin enough that you could feel that there was no pulse?"

"Yeah."

"Okay. All right. And when what happened again. Tell us, tell us what happened right after that."

"Right after?"

"Mm-hm."

"Well, I went into the kitchen, got the phone and the cup, put the phone in her, put the cup in him and then I left."

"Were you tired?"

"Yeah."

"Did you take a drink of water?"

"I don't think so," Marsh said. "No I didn't."

"You don't think so? No. Did you sit down?"

"Did I what?"

"Sit down. Rest."

"Uh, I think I just left."

"Okay. Um, carried the knife away, cell phone, didn't lose anything. Did you duct tape anything? We heard about duct tape at one point."

"No, I didn't use duct tape."

"I'm not talking about on them. I'm talking about on yourself, your clothing or anything like that."

"Yeah. No."

"Okay. Um, take any pictures?"

"No."

"Did it tempt you to take some pictures?"

"Yeah, but I figured it was a bad idea."

"Bad idea?"

"Yeah."

"Okay. So no pictures? Did you wish later that you had?"

"Yeah."

"Even thought it was a bad idea? Why? What would that have given you, Dan?"

"Gratification," Marsh said.

"Relive it?"

"Yeah."

"I think you mentioned the word 'trophy' in regard to having the clothing there."

"No, it was a souvenir."

"Okay, souvenir, in what way? Describe to me what that means to you."

"It's kind of a little memento and a constant reminder of what happened," Marsh said. "Just so I can see it and kind of relive it."

"So what, and one of the items in particular? Or just kind of all of them together?"

"Just all of them."

"So the knife's not more than the jacket, which is more than the ski mask?"

"No, I washed the knife cause, well, I felt like I should do that."

"Where, where did you do that?"

"In the sink."

"Back at your mom's house. Okay. All right. Um, since that time, has it been building in you?"

"Yes."

"Have you thought about what you were going to do next?"

"Yes."

"And what's that?"

"Uh, kind of basically do the same thing only with a different mask and different gloves, different jacket," Marsh said. "And instead of breaking in, I figured I'd get somebody when they're alone at night out in the street or out somewhere. Just find somebody alone and night and beat him to death with a baseball bat."

"Okay. Did you have anybody in mind?"

"No."
"Had you actually gone looking for someone?"
"Yeah."
"When was that?"
"I don't remember," Marsh said. "Done it a couple of times."
"A couple of times since two months ago? Did you have any contacts? Did you think, find anybody you think would be likely?"
"No."
"What time of day was this when you'd go out?"
"Like between one and four in the morning."
"All right," Campion said. "Did you ever have any problem getting out, coming back in? Your mom ever catch on?"
"No."
"And during any of this time, was anybody else living in the house with you and your mom?"
"No."
"Okay. So, nobody, did you try it with anybody? Hit them once and they got away or anything like that?"
"Nothing like that."
"Baseball bat at the house, too?"
"Yeah, but I didn't use it."
"Right."
"Yeah."
"Why the baseball bat instead of a knife?"
"I don't know," Marsh said. "I wanted to mix it up."
"Mix it up."
"And also I figured if one of them was a blunt object and neither one was a break-in with a knife, it wouldn't be correlated, you know?"
"Wouldn't be connected," Campion said. "Was that in Davis, or was that somewhere else?"
"Was what?"
"Was that in Davis, or would that have been somewhere else?"
"It probably would have been in Davis."
"Do you have access to a car?"
"Yeah, but I have to like steal it from my mom, and that's. . ."
"Higher risk?"
"Yeah."

"So you go other couple of times, or just random times went out the last couple of months with the baseball bat?"

"Pretty much."

"How about going back before the older couple? Had you gotten close to anybody else in the times we were talking about with your mom's girlfriend and the school incidents, people at school?"

"No."

"Was there anybody particular at school that you had targeted that you thought was really, pissed you off and that you want to take care of?"

"No really."

"Did you ever think about going into the school with a gun and, like doing a Columbine type thing?"

"Well, yeah," Marsh said, "but I didn't have a gun."

"But that would have been different because you would have like, you said, not probably survived that one?"

"Well, yeah, didn't care."

"At that point you didn't care. Okay. Do you feel any sense of relief now, Dan?"

"No."

"Okay."

"Uh, not at all, actually."

"Well, I think you did the right thing. I think that there was, it happened one way or another."

"Well, yeah, you got my DNA, and you got my phone."

"Okay. What else?"

"What else what?"

"What else can you share?" Campion said. "Things that you remember we talked about. Remember when we were first starting, about the people who, um, sexually attracted to young kids. They didn't, don't want that. It's not that you feel that way about young kids, but that is kind of the analogy."

"In a way, yeah. I don't want to feel the way I feel. I don't want to have the thoughts I have. I don't want to have the dreams that I dream. I don't."

"Dan, which came first? Was it the website, like the bestgore.com stuff. Did that fuel it, or did you .. ?"

"It actually kind of helped defuel it 'cause it was kind of a way to indulge in it without actually committing a crime. But that wasn't enough."

"Okay. How long have you been on that website?"

"For like a year."

"And were there any other ones? That's the only one? Okay. Any other magazines, other media, stuff like that would have attracted you? When you've accessed those websites, what's your means of, uh, access for your media?"

"We have a computer."

"Laptop? Tower? Which one?"

"Laptop."

"Laptop. Is it yours or is there more than one in the house?"

"It's mine."

"Does your mom have a separate one? Anybody else have another computer that's there that belongs to somebody else? All right. Did you ever use your mom's for anything?"

"No."

"In regards to this? Research, anything like that?"

"No."

"Did you ever look up on the computer and do research on psychopaths?"

"Yeah."

"Why did you do that?"

"I wanted to, I don't know," Marsh said. "I looked up sociopath and psychopath 'cause I always found it fascinating, and the more I aged, the more I can relate. Because I don't feel sympathy for other people, at all. Don't feel empathy for them, and whether I like it that or not, it's the way it is. Just like I want to hurt people. I want to kill people but I don't want to want that. I wish it wasn't that way."

"Again, very well spoken," Campion said. "You want to hurt people but you wish that you didn't want to."

"Yeah."

"You don't want to want that."

"Yeah. I, I don't want to be the way I am, but. . ."

"There's no way around it, though, right?"

"Because it's the way I am, and I'm it whether I like it or not."

"Okay. And that's the case. That's the truth, that's the science, that's the research, that's the reality on the ground here. So again, you're not alone, for whatever that's worth. Um, I wish I had better news for you about whether that could be changed or cured or anyway different."

"Right."

"Can you see it being different?"

"Some aspects of it."

"Which aspect?"

"I think that I can be treated for being on this aisle, because I know that I can't be the first one. I don't know, obviously I know that there has to be some sort of treatment for it, but as for the no sympathy or empathy, I don't think I can change that."

"Do you ever remember a time when you did have it?"

"I do, yeah," Marsh said. "I wasn't always like this."

"What age, where you thing that changed?"

"Maybe 14. It just, it just disappeared."

"Really? Pretty suddenly?"

"Yeah, it just, you know, it just kind of crept up on me. I just started caring less and less and then I just wasn't there."

"Okay. And the cat thing that we talked about with Alvaro. Was that you?"

"No, he actually did choke a cat to death. I wasn't lying about that. He actually did. He has hurt animals. That part was real but, yeah, I have hurt animals."

"How old were you when you started doing that?"

"Uh, 11."

"And what kind of animals?"

"We had pet birds, and well, the first thing I did was I killed them and I blamed the cat."

"Then blamed the cat. So what did you move to next?"

"Then I killed a neighborhood stray cat."

"How did you do that?"

"I snapped its neck."

"Were you by yourself for those?"

"I never killed an animal or killed anything with anyone."

"Wouldn't occur to you it wouldn't make sense?" Campion said. "Most people understand. How many animals would you say that you killed over the course of your adolescence?"

"Like seven."

"Seven? All right. Any experience with arson, with fire?"

"I haven't. I haven't been an arsonist, but I like fire."

"Got an attraction to it, but you never started a fire, just to see what happened? See it burn?"

"I never burned anything of anyone else's."

"What would you burn, of yourself, or your own, or your family's?"

"I'd just play with the fireplace. I'd burn stuff and I would burn paper whenever I got the opportunity and just I like fire."

"What's the attraction?" Campion said. "What do you like about it?"

"I don't know. It's like a beautiful form of destruction."

"Does it satisfy the rage, satisfy the need?"

"I don't know. It's just calling."

"Calling? Okay. Um, the other thing that we see sometimes in adolescence is the bed wetting at pretty advanced age. Did you ever have any of that?"

"Yeah."

"To what age? Or is it still?"

"No, it's not a problem. It stopped. Uh, it was between, I don't now if it was five or six, maybe seven. It was in that time period, though, between five and seven, but it was finally stopped."

"Was it a pretty nightly occurrence?"

"Yeah, it was."

"Or was it night, I guess I should have asked first. Was it at night?"

"Yeah, it didn't stop until I was like seven."

"Pretty, um, cause friction in your family? Your mom, your dad, give you a hard time about it?"

"Yeah."

"Did they do anything in particular to try to get you to stop?"

"Not really," Marsh said. "It just stopped at some point and it like happened every now and then but it hasn't happened in like probably since I was ten. Just stopped."

"Okay. Tell us again how far back the dreams of hurting people started."

"Started like around the time I was 14."

"And what would the dreams be like? What was a typical dream?"

"It started out with I'd just be dressed in all black in a hood and

I'd wander this big city that I've never seen before, and I'd just kill whoever was on the street. It evolved from there to, and it got to the point where, I don't know why, but I have a dream that the people I was killing were the people I care about and things I was doing to them and to other people as well."

"Okay. So that, that showed up in your dreams?"

"Yeah."

"Would you think about that during the day as much?"

"Um, the only thing sort of like thinking about it is that when I'd see someone I'd just get those images and thoughts, but it's the difference between a thought and a desire."

"Talk more, a little bit more about that," Campion said. "What, how, are they related and how did they occur, in your experience?"

"I've had these thoughts, but that doesn't mean I want to have them or want to act on them."

"Right. So you have the thought that occurs to you that you're. . ."

"I have no desire to harm the people that I care about. I can't help it. That tears my mind, though."

"Okay. So it did at night, a subconscious thing when you're dreaming?"

"Yeah."

"Was that a regular occurrence?"

"It's become one."

"When you were awake, even though didn't really want to think that, did you ever formulate a plan to do that to any of your parents, or to any of your family members?"

"Yeah," Marsh said. "But not with my friends."

"Tell us about your family members? Who were you thinking about?"

"It started with my sister, 'cause she's always been a bitch."

"Yeah, I could tell you didn't like her too much," Campion said. "What kind of fantasy did you have about that?"

"I wanted to stab her to death. My mom, I wanted to smother her with a pillow. My dad, I just wanted to beat him to death."

"Okay. So those were the dreams, the dreams or the fantasies? What, how did you get to the point where you were able to think about this during the day? Day dream?"

"Yeah, it happens all the time."

"Pretty much all, all the time. So you're sitting in school and thinking about it."

"Yeah. It's one of the reasons that I struggle so much in school. I'm not stupid. I can do the work. I just, my mind is so preoccupied with everything else, and that mixed with depression and anxiety is kind of a whole clusterfuck of problems."

"Recipe for disaster."

"Pretty much."

"All right. But not your friends. You haven't thought, had those thoughts and fantasies."

"Well, I've had the thoughts, and well, I wouldn't call 'em fantasies just thoughts. I've had fantasies about others."

"You've had fantasies about others? About killing others?"

"Yeah. I have," Marsh said. "It's kind of a constant thing."

"So pretty much constant, all the time, you're, it occurs to you that you can kill this person, you can kill that person."

"Yeah."

"And in these thoughts, Dan, and stabbing mostly? Beating? All the above?"

"It's actually just kind of a mixture."

"A mixture," Campion said. "Okay. Again, not significantly different than everybody I've talked to, who are kind of afflicted with the same thing."

"Okay."

"Well, Dan, thank you for helping us understand a little bit more and about what happened. Otherwise. Ariel, anything else you'd like to talk about?"

"Not at the moment," Pineda said. "I'll be right back."

"Sure," said Campion, who turned again to Daniel Marsh.

"What questions you have for me?"

"Was I really screwed either way?"

"Mm-hm."

"Okay," Marsh said. "Good."

"Yeah. We would have found all that stuff, Dan. We would have tested it. It would have come back with blood on it."

"I know."

"It would have been the victims' blood."

Marsh suddenly perked up.

"Was there actually DNA left back there, though? At the crime scene?"

"There are unknown DNA profiles. I don't know if they are yours or not. We'll find out."

"Hm."

"Could be people, other people in the house we don't know about that we don't have identified. We haven't compared these profiles with. If there was, if you think you might have made a small error, at the house?"

"I don't think I did," Marsh said. "That's why I was, thinking."

"No, it was, it was a very well executed crime," Campion said. "No doubt about it."

"Thank you," said Marsh, with a laugh louder than before.

"Clearly, you're a smart guy," Campion said. "But for these afflictions I think you would have a different life. No doubt."

"Yeah, pretty much done now."

"Well I don't know what the future of the science and the psychology and all of that will hold," Campion said. "I don't know. The brain technology, the brain scanning, all of that has come so far in the 25 years I've been doing this has come so far in helping us understand what's going on. So if there's research in that way that there's maybe somewhere down the road, I don't think that is right now but maybe in five or ten years. Maybe we'll be further uh down in terms of treatment. Because I'm firmly convinced, Dan, that it's electro-chemical in the brain, and biology in the brain. It's where it starts. Oh, I wanted to ask you, um, video games, you mentioned video games."

"Yeah."

"What role did that play in this whole thing, for you?"

"For me, it's an escape. You know, you can get sucked into a different reality, a different world that isn't this one."

"Mm-hm."

"It's just kind of, yeah just an escape."

"And the killing part of the video games? Is that part of the escape? Is that necessary for escape?"

"Yeah, it helps," Marsh said.

"Kind of that um, scene you were describing, you walking outside of your mom's house, and just kind of walking and walking and walking, kind of reminded me of that one video game you were describing earlier. Where you were kind of, you know, you were going through and you were doing these different tasks and solving these puzzles and things like that. Is that a real connection, or is that just. . ?"

"I think that was just a coincidence."

"Okay. Tell me about Lamb of God. Are they here in Davis?"

"No, kind of, they're pretty big."

"What kind of music?"

"Metal? Uh."

"Any of the metal music?" Campion said. "I know if you were listening to country and western music that wouldn't make you any different, you know, as far as what your interests are, what your mind is. But, um, what I guess I asked you about the video games? What about the metal music? Any effect that you?"

"It's, um, it's another escape for me. It's another way to cope, 'cause it's really peaceful to me. I actually fall asleep listening to like Death Metal."

"Really?"

"Yeah. It's weird. It's calming."

"Okay, that's a new one on me. I hadn't heard that before. So Lamb of God, huh. Any particular lyrics you recall off the top of your head with them?"

Marsh wore a dark Lamb of God T-shirt.

"These guys?"

"Yeah. Uh, yeah, uh, there's one thing that the guy says in the beginning of the song that I always liked was, 'Whoever appeals to the law against his fellow man is either a fool or a coward. Whoever cannot take care of himself without that law is both. For a wounded man shall say to his assailant. If I live I will kill you. If I die, you are forgiven. Such is the rule of honor.'"

"Wow," Campion said. "Okay."

"And there's actually some really beautiful metal lyrics and music that's just, it's just like regular music. There's a bunch of crap that you have to sift through to find the good stuff."

"Yeah. What are some of the other favorites?"

"Lyrics or bands?"

"Both."

"Bands, um, Slipknot, Chelsea Grin, Suicide Silence, Lamb of God. Those are my main four."

"All right. Well it's, do you go to concerts, or any more of ?"

"Yeah."

"Spotify and concerts."

"Both of them," Marsh said. "Spotify and concerts."

"So, as a 16-year-old, um, juvenile hall, I don't know anything about there and Yolo County. It's probably a pretty sure bet that you're not gonna be messing with other kids at this point, anyway. So I don't know how long it will take to navigate through the process."

"So when am I? Am I going there? Like after this?"

"Yeah. Yeah we have to. . ."

"Can I eat something? I haven't eaten all day."

"Um we might have some cold pizza in the station somewhere. What would you like? Candy bar?"

"Um, I'm kind of a health nut."

"You're a health nut," Campion said.

"In a way."

"So fruit, vegetables, that kind of stuff?"

"Yeah, do you have any fruit? That'd be like awesome."

"Okay, let me see if I can. . ."

"Also, is there a bathroom I can use?"

"Uh, yeah, although I don't work here all the time, so just hold on for a second. I just want to make sure that we can find somebody who knows their way around here. Hey Lieutenant? Can I borrow you for a sec? Um he needs to go to the bathroom, and um, he's asking for something to eat around here, kind of not candy bars or pizza, stuff that I usually eat, obviously, but maybe something a bit more healthy?"

"Like a Subway sandwich?" said a woman.

"Like a Subway sandwich or something?"

"Mm-hm," Marsh said.

A cop raised the prospect of a ham and cheese sandwich.

"Are you a vegetarian?" Campion said.

"No."

"All right. I can work on that for you."

Campion tasked a cop to go along with Marsh.

"So is this one of those two-way mirrors?" Marsh said. "Are there like people on the other side?"

"That's kind of old school. Um. Yeah."

"We don't use it a whole lot," a cop said.

"Oh."

"They always see you."

"And invariably somebody coughs or something like that," Campion said. "There's nobody back there, you want to look?"

"I don't really care," Marsh said. "Just interested."

"All right," Campion said. "Let me work on food and see what we can rustle up, okay?"

Campion departed. A cop told Marsh to have a seat while he found someone to accompany him. Alone in the room, he pounded the wall and said:

"What the fuck am I doing here?"

Chapter 11

"She begged me to stop."

After his bathroom break, Chris Campion returned.

"Okay, the only thing we can find that's not pizza, candy bars, um, remotely healthy are these kind of things."

He showed what appeared to be a bar of some kind.

"Is that something you want to give a try?"

"Why not?" Marsh said.

"Chocolate, peanut butter, protein something or other. Okay and of course I've got a whole list of things they're asking for follow-up, based on being over at your mom's house."

Ariel Pineda returned to the room.

"Uh, one of which is, I guess there's several knives in the garage. Um, we're gonna take 'em all and have them tested anyway. And can you describe more specifically the Buck knife?"

"Um, black and gray handle."

"Black and gray handle. How long is it?"

"It's labeled, Buck Knife."

"Oh, it's actually, so it's not just a buck-type knife. It's labeled that."

"It's like on the blade it says the Buck Knife, and it's in a black sheath."

"Oh."

Marsh held his hands apart.

"Blade's only like, that long."

"So what do you think? Like six inches, maybe?"

"Yeah, around that."

"Okay. All right," Campion said. Is there going to be anything on those other knives that are in the garage?"

"No."

"Okay. There's a roll of duct tape in your room. You have like an abnormal interest in duct tape that you know that whole thing about a thousand and one uses. Uh, many of them are used in our business, so anything that duct tape was used for?"

"No, it's just duct tape," Marsh said with another laugh.

"Okay. So not going to be hairs or anything on that, you know, would be connected to something else we haven't talked about already?"

"Uh-uh."

"Okay, um, the screen, you kind of described it, but I was asked to, cause it's just, it was just on that iPad. So if I'm going to draw, just a rectangular shape here, could you just kind of dot where you cut around the screen please? How are those things? Are they good?"

"Not bad."

"Okay. Have the other one, Dan. It would probably not agree with my constitution."

"So who know, um well, who knows."

"Okay. All right. So it, and is that, Dan, where the window looks like this? Like the bottom is down this way?"

"No."

"Or is the bottom like down this way?"

Marsh indicated the places.

"Okay. Gotcha," Campion said. "Thank you. All right, the screen and then inside the house we noticed that the place next to a chair, I think in that room with all the mirrors that you described, and there was a book on a, like a side table or little hutch or something and then there was a rag urn on there. Do you remember anything about that having anything to do with you?"

"No."

"Okay, similarly in there, there was some money found in the house, but there was some thought that maybe some money had been missing."

"I had nothing to do with money," Marsh said, with a note of pride.

"Right, I know that wasn't any motivation, but did you happen to see some and just grab it and go?"

"No."

"Okay. The way that you got over there, I mean, Ariel and I heard you say you kind of found you're outside of your mom's house, middle of the night, wee hours of the morning, and you kind of found yourself over there."

"Well, I walked around that direction, so I headed down the end of the cul-de-sac and then down the next street that was there. After checking all those houses, that was the first one that actually had an open access point."

"Okay. So you didn't leave your mom's house with those two people in mind?"

"Not really."

"Not even that area?"

"No," Marsh said. "I just kind of walked around."

"How many houses would you say you checked, like the knobs, the doors and looked at the screens and so forth?"

"A lot. About like 50."

Campion repeated the number.

"I don't know. Checked a lot."

"Mostly in the area around Cowell there?"

"Yeah, it was kind of spread out. They had these apartments by my house called the Renaissance Apartments or something and I checked there and then from there I went back into the back path and just went around there and just kind of went around, one to two-mile radius from my house."

"Like how much?"

"Like a two or three mile radius of my house."

"Oh, so you were walking a lot."

"Yeah."

"All right," Campion said. "Anybody run into you, you know, any close calls, anything like that?"

"No, I was actually, I didn't see a single person that night, except . . ."

"Really?"

"Yeah."

"Wow, cars? No cars?"

Marsh indicated that there had been no cars.

"And what time of day do you think it was, like they're actually found there?"

"Like three."

"Okay. And what time do you think you would have gotten back to your mom's house?"

"Around four."

"Okay. Because from there to your mom's house if you, what do you do? You come over the bridge and, how did you? Do you remember how you got back?"

"Yeah. Just walked right over it."

"Walked right over that bridge. What is that bridge called?"

Pineda knew the territory.

"Well, it's a couple ways back to Lillard from Cowell," the detective said. "Did you go back on Cowell or did you go back like, um, the back way?"

"I just went, took the streets."

"Okay, so you didn't have, didn't cross the freeway?"

"I wasn't on the freeway."

"How did you get over the freeway, I mean, I should remember?"

"I didn't."

Pineda explained that Marsh's mother's residence was south of the freeway. So was the crime scene, where Campion directed the conversation.

"Um, when she woke up and you said you think she was planning on going to the bathroom?"

"I figured as much, since the bathroom is like right there. She was right there, getting up, facing that way."

"Okay. Do you remember her saying anything to you? You said that she was, told us that she was screaming some."

"No, she gasped and then she started screaming and, she didn't scream that long after."

"Okay," said Campion. "Did she say anything to you, though? Sometimes people. . ."

"Uh, she begged me to stop," Marsh said.

"Like what did she say?"

"Please stop, please, please stop."

"All right. Did you say anything to her?"

Marsh indicated he did not.

"All right. And did he say anything to you?"

"He didn't have a chance," Marsh said. "I kind of just went, got his neck."

"Okay. All right. Thoughts, questions that occurred to you while you were gone trying to hunt down something that wasn't revolting to you?"

"Um, yeah, who have you, who all knows what is going on right now?"

"Well, I don't know, 'cause we've been in here mostly."

"Are you thinking about like your family or something?" Pineda said.

"Family, friends."

"There's been searching going on at your mom's house, so she's aware," Campion said. "And there had been searching going on at your dad's house. I don't know if he came back. I'm not sure that he's aware of the searching going on. As far as anybody that we would tell that didn't already know, or heard from other people, who heard from other people, that doesn't happen. We don't go out and tell people about this kind of stuff."

"Thanks for the . . ."

"You're welcome," Pineda said.

"It's okay," Campion added.

"Yeah, not bad."

"So we don't do that. I mean, your mother and your father will know, sometime fairly soon. Do you think they're going to be shocked?"

"Yeah."

"Or not so much?"

"Probably."

"Do you think they will?" Campion said. "What's the real reason that your dad moved, Dan?"

"Like I told you. Like, I wasn't bullshitting."

"That was true?"

"Yeah."

"That he was afraid for his own safety?"

"Uh, well that was a little bit of it, and then the landlady actually was dead. They were actually rushing to move."

"Okay."

"I didn't bullshit as much as you think I did," Marsh said.

"I appreciate that."

"What else? Ariel?"

"Yeah, I think you shared everything," the detective said. "My only curious thought was, that particular night, you had such a buildup, and was it just because of those things you have been telling us, or was it something?"

"Just, it was years of buildup, nothing, no event happened for me to just be like, all right, I'm doing it. It just, it got unbearable."

"Okay."

Campion had more questions of his own.

"I don't want to insult you at all," the FBI man said, "but there is sometimes a sexual aspect to this. Present in your case at all? Did you have any sexual excitation?"

"No."

"You thought for a second there."

"Well, not in this case," Marsh said. "I think I could if, it would depend on who I was killing, though."

"Okay, talk to us some more about that."

"If it was someone I was attracted to, then, yeah, it'd be sexual, but you know, they were really old and gross."

"But the act of killing did, didn't give you sexual?"

"A little bit. I don't know, I was more caught up in the euphoria."

"Okay."

"Um, back, your dad lived there. Did you know the residents of the apartment you went into? Did you really know who lived there?"

"Um, I met them once before but it was a long time ago," Marsh said. "I didn't even remember."

"We had talked about that I think at one point when you had stepped out, that he had met them when his dad moved into that place."

"Got it," Pineda said.

"And they had actually had him and his dad inside the place, and shown around, talked to them a bit. But that wasn't on your mind when you went back?"

"No, I wasn't thinking about . . ."

"Just to make sure."

"That at all."

"Did you have a picture of them, a mental picture of them when you went in there?"

"No, not at all."

"So it could have been?"

"Could have been. . ."

"A young couple," Campion said. "It could have been a single woman. It could have been?"

"Could have been anybody," Marsh said.

"Anybody, yeah."

"And the idea obviously the cell phone and the cup," Pineda said. "And you went back to the kitchen?"

"Yeah, honestly," Marsh said. "I just kind of wanted to fuck with you guys."

"Where'd you find the cell phone?"

"It was next to the phone with a cord. They had a cord phone. I think on the wall and next to it there was like that one plugged into a charger."

"In the kitchen also?" said Pineda. "Okay."

"And then the cup?"

"It was like in the kitchen, just on the counter."

"Just on the counter," Campion said, "like it had been washed or, it was next to the sink?"

"It was next to the sink."

"Not in the cupboard or anything?" said Campion. "Okay. Well, let me write down some of those metal bands that you were talking about."

"All right."

Marsh showed enthusiasm for the task.

"So we've got Lamb of God on your shirt there."

"Slipknot, Chelsea Grin."

"Chelsea Grin. G-R-I-N?"

"Yeah. Uh, Suicide Silence. Do you want me just to list a bunch of them?"

"Your favorite ones," Campion said. "The ones that mean something to you, you think are good, that somebody who's obviously a lot older than you, that uh, if I wanted to listen to metal, to see, maybe I haven't given it a fair shot. So if you say that you can actually relax to it."

"Chelsea has some of the more melodic stuff," Marsh said. "Uh, Born of Osiris."

"Okay. That gives me some good ones. And that lyric, that you quoted to me, what was the name of that song?"

"Omerta," Marsh said, "like O-M-E-R-T-A."

"And that is Lamb of God?"

"Yeah."

"Do you know what Omertà is?"

"I do not actually."

"It's the oath the Mafia takes when they join the Mafia, to never, never talk outside of their group."

"Hmm." Marsh said. "Cool."

"Dan, thanks for that," Campion said. After a pause, the FBI man said:

"I'm kind of debating whether to ask this next question, Dan."

"All right."

"You mentioned that pretty much everybody you meet you have thoughts about killing them and how you would kill them."

"Yeah."

"So how would you kill me?"

"Just a lot of ways," Marsh said with little hesitation.

"But I mean, that you've thought of so far in the couple hours that we've spent together here."

"Um, choking you to death with your tie."

"Okay."

"Uh, beating your face into the mirror until it broke and using the glass to cut your arteries. Uh, gouging out your eyes and just smashing your face into the wall. Nothing personal."

"I don't take it personal."

"Okay. It's just. . ."

"It's just, that's what happens when you meet somebody, when you're thinking when there's that time when you . . ."

"Yeah, it's involuntary. It's just something that just happens. It's like breathing. You don't think about it. It just happens."

"Can't control it."

"I couldn't if I wanted to," Marsh said, "and I do want to."

"Well, like I was saying, there might be a day when you can. There might be a day when science comes far enough, medicine comes far enough, where you can. I hope for your sake and for our society's that

that happens. Let me ask you, Dan, are you feeling right now as far as suicide? Are you thinking any thoughts like you were before?"

"Not really," Marsh said. "I'm just, I don't really know what I'm feeling."

"Okay. I really hope you don't try it anymore. I think that there's hope, possibility, maybe this can come to an end at some point. That's not that, it's not death for you, in the near future. But Ariel and I sincerely wish you the best going through this, and I know that maybe sounds a little weird, too. We would cure you if we can, we would heal you if we can. But right now we can't so we have to do the next best thing that we have to do."

"What is that?"

"We just have to keep you away from other people so you don't have the opportunities to hurt anybody else."

"So when am I going wherever I'm going?"

"I think there's nothing else," Pineda said. "We don't have anything else. Start the process."

Campion looked at Marsh.

"Are you ready?"

"Pretty much."

"Okay I have to get you down to another part of the building," Pineda said. "We'll go through the back way, less visible, and start the processing. Fill out the paperwork and we'll go from there."

"All right."

"Okay?"

"Can I have my shoes?" Marsh said. "Is that really necessary?"

"Yeah," Pineda said. "Potential evidence."

"Find like . . ."

"It's amazing," Campion said, "What kind of blood stuff, what kind of stuff ends up on shoes."

"I don't know," Marsh said. "I figure you're gonna have enough."

Pineda brandished shackles.

"Okay, while we walk through the building, I'm gonna have to put these on you and we'll take them off when we get to the other end. Okay?"

"All right."

"Oh wait," Campion said. "Ariel, before you hook up, I want to shake his hand."

"Cool," Marsh said.
"Well, your gonna undo it, right?" Campion said
"Yeah," said Pineda.
The detective freed Marsh's hand. Chris Campion shook it.
"All right," the FBI man said. "I'll walk with you guys."
"Take a right," Pineda said, as the three left the room.

Chapter 12

Tortured Justice

The interview at the Davis Police Department lasted more than four hours and yielded some 40,000 words, but "torture" was not among them. Even so, the charges against Daniel Marsh included a special circumstance for the infliction of torture in the commission of murder. On June 19, 2013, Daniel Marsh pleaded not guilty to the charges.

In Marsh's preliminary hearing on September 13, 2013, the crowded gallery heard Davis police officers testify about finding the mutilated bodies of Claudia Maupin and Oliver "Chip" Northup. Yolo County deputy coroner Gina Moya testified that both died from multiple stab wounds. According to the autopsy report, the murderer had stabbed Claudia Maupin 67 times and Oliver Northup 61 times. That drew a gasp from the gallery, and so did Moya's testimony that both bodies had been "eviscerated."

Detective Ariel Pineda told the court that Claudia Maupin had pleaded with Marsh to stop, but Marsh kept on stabbing because "she just wouldn't die." The stabbing "just felt right," Marsh had told the detective. The killings gave him a high that lasted a week, and he had already sought to kill others.

Ronald Johnson, Marsh's public defender, sought to have the confession tossed but Judge David Reed rejected that bid. In the ensuing trial, described at length in *Exceptional Depravity: Dan Who Likes Dark and Double Murder in Davis, California,* Daniel Marsh did not testify, but jurors did get to hear him. In their opening statement, prosecutors played the section of the interview where Marsh said the murders "felt amazing," "pure happiness," and "the most exhilarating, enjoyable feeling I've ever felt." The jury saw that episode again during playback of the entire interview, and other trial testimony filled in some of the blanks.

According to one friend, Daniel Marsh "liked to torture," a subject he discussed openly with psychologists, who found him a "sexual sadist." Testimony from forensic pathologist Dr. Mark Super, and his autopsy report, makes it clear that Marsh did in fact torture Claudia Maupin and Oliver "Chip" Northup.

"It was well executed crime," Chris Campion said, and young Dan "almost got away with it." The killer duly confessed but in a couple of ways he did get away with it.

In September 2014 the Yolo County jury found Marsh guilty of two counts of first-degree murder. The jury also found that he had been sane when he committed the murders. On December 12, 2014, Judge David Reed sentenced Daniel Marsh to 52 years to life in state prison. He took two lives but gets to preserve his own, but there was more to it still.

The jury also found true the enhancements for deadly weapon, lying in wait, and torture. The enhancement for use of a deadly weapon added only one year to each 25-year sentence for murder. On the other hand, the enhancements for lying in wait and torture added *zero* time to the sentence.

After stops at Chino and Ironwood state prison, Daniel Marsh, 18, is inmate AW0819 at the Richard J. Donovan Correctional Center near San Diego, a "minimum support facility" with vocational, academic and industrial programs. The inmate will be eligible for parole at age 42, not 46, or later. So in a real sense, the exceptionally depraved double murderer got away with torture.

Appendix: Autopsy Reports

Maupin: Claudia Maureen. Postmortem Date: 04-15-2013. Time: 16:00. Place of death: Usual residence. Date found: 04-14-2013. Time: 22:01. Age: 76. Sex: Female. Height: 65 in. Weight: 180 lb.

Autopsy findings

1. Stab and superficial incised wounds (6) of face.
    A.   Two stab wounds of left cheek penetrate into oral cavity.

2. Stab-incised wound (1) of right neck.
    A.   Incisions of tongue, thyroid and larynx.
    B.   Maximum depth: 8 cm. (3 in.)

3. Stab and superficial incised wounds (5) of anterolateral left neck.
    A.   Maximum depth: 8 cm (3 in.)

4. Complex stab-incised wound (1) of left lateral shoulder.
    A. One wound track courses lateral to medial exiting the left pectoral area.
    B.   One would track courses downward exiting medial left upper arm
    C. Maximum depth 12.5 cm (5 in.)

5. Multiple Stab wounds (28) of abdomen.
    A.   Most penetrate through abdominal wall into peritoneal cavity.
    B.   Perforation of liver.
    C.   Perforations of pancreas.
    D.   Perforations of stomach, small bowel, mesentery and omentum.
    E.   Transection of right colon.
    F.   Hemoperitoneum (100 ml).

6. Large complex stab-incised wound (1) of left abdomen.
   A. Omentum and colon herniate from the wound.
   B. Cell phone found in the abdomen associated with this wound.

7. Stab wounds (8) of left lateral chest wall.
   A. Perforations of left chest wall into left lung.
   B. Left hemothorax (550 ml)
   C. Penetration into left breast.
   D. Maximum measured depth: 10.5 cm (4 in.)

8. Stab wounds (10) of left arm, some perforating.
   A. incision of proximal left radius.

9. Long vertical stab-incised wound (1) of medial right thigh.
   A. Stab wound depth: 11 cm. (4 ½ in)

10. Stab-incised wound (1) of medial right thigh.
    A. Maximum depth: 11.5 cm (4 ½ in.)

11. Stab wounds (2) of anterior left thigh.
    A. Maximum depth, 11. 5 cm (4 ½ in.)

12. Stab wounds (3) of left upper back.
    A. Maximum Depth, 11. 5 cm (4 ½ in.)

Cause of death: Multiple stab wounds.

Opinion: The decedent sustained at least 67 separate stab and incised wounds.

Mark A. Super, M.D. forensic pathologist. June 23, 2013.

The autopsy is conducted at the Yolo County Sheriff-Coroner's Morgue Facility in Woodland, Ca. Investigator: Deputy Coroner G. Moya. Witnesses: Investigators T. Souza and R. Strange, Yolo County District Attorney's office; Sergeant M. Munoz and CSI Officer M. Alfaro, Davis Police Department; Deputy Coroner G. Moya and Intern J. Foster, Yolo County Sheriff-Coroner's Office. Autopsy assistant: S. Barnes.

Evidence of Injury

Coursing along the anterior base of the nose is a horizontal 2 cm long incised wound (labeled #1) that extends just through the skin. On the tip of the nose is a 0.6 cm superficial cut (labeled #2). Lateral to the left nasal ala is an obliquely oriented 2.5 cm long superficial incised wound (labeled #3). This lacks any evidence of hemorrhage. On the lower left cheek is an obliquely oriented 1.4 cm long stab wound (labeled #4) composed of an inferior/anterior blunt end opposed by a pointed end. The wound path perforates the skin and subcutis of he left cheek and penetrates into the oral cavity. The wound path is left to right and slightly downward. Lateral to the left angle of the mouth is a horizontal 2.2 cm long stab wound (labeled #5) composed of a posterior/lateral blunt end opposed by a pointed end. This wound perforates the skin and subcutis of he lower left cheek and penetrates into the oral cavity, oriented left to right. Extending from the pointed end into the corner of the mouth is a 1.2 cm linear abrasion. Just above the wound is a 1.8 cm jagged linear abrasion-superficial cut. Also at the left angle of the mouth is a 0.6 cm linear abrasion. Anterior to the left ear is an obliquely oriented 2.5 cm long stab wound (labeled #6) composed of anterior blunt end opposed by a pointed end. The wound path perforates the skin and subcutis of the left side of the head and impacts the ramus of the mandible. The wound path is straight left to right and horizontal.

On the right anterolateral neck is a chevron-shaped vertically oriented 7 cm long stab-incised wound (labeled #12). The right lateral edge is beveled. The superior half of he wound is an incision that extends just into the subcutis. The lower half is a stab wound oriented front to back and upward, up to 8 cm deep, extending into the neck where it incises the thyroid gland and larynx, incises the tongue, and impacts the cervical spine. Another path from this same stab round goes downward and medially through the right sternocleidomastoid muscle and into the supraclavicular space.

Multiple stab and incised wounds are on the anterior and left lateral neck. This includes an oblique 1.7 cm long stab wound (labeled #7) near the left angle of the mouth, oriented from upper posterior to lower lateral, which perforates the skin of the left nick and penetrates left to right, slightly upward and front to back for a depth of 9 cm. Distinct neck structures are not noted to be injured along this path but I cannot rule out that right-sided laryngeal injuries are due to this wound, also. Below that on the left neck is a chevron-shaped 15 cm long superficial incised wound (labeled #8) that focally extends into subcutis. The anterior end of this wound is jagged. Lateral to that is a horizontal 2 cm long superficial stab-incised wound (labeled #10) that does not extend completely through skin. Below that is a horizontal 1.6 cm long superficial stab-incised wound (labeled #9) that does not extend completely through skin. Just above that wound is a 3.2 cm long horizontal linear abrasion. The most inferior wound of this group is a 1.7 cm long stab wound (labeled #11) compose of a right lateral blunt end opposed by a pointed end. This extends front to back and downward for a depth of 7 cm.

On the lateral left shoulder is a 7 x 6 cm, complex, somewhat stellate shaped stab-incised wound (labeled #14). Two large gaping components of this wound extend upward and one extends forward. Multiple stab wound paths extend from this wound. One of these paths extends medially, exiting the upper left pectoral skin through a vertical 2.6 cm long stab exit defect (labeled #13). This 6 cm long stab wound path is straight left to right and slightly back to front. Another track extends downward, slightly front to back and lateral to medial from wound #14 on the lateral left shoulder for a distance of 12.5 cm and then exits the skin through a 2.2 cm stab defect (labeled #63) on the medial left upper arm near the axilia. The exit defect has a posterior blunt end opposed by a pointed end.

On the left mid-abdomen is a complex Y-shaped jagged stab-incised wound (labeled #35). The wound measures 20 cm in maximum length and gapes to 6 cm. Jagged defects along the edge suggest the wound is composed of multiple interconnecting stab and incised wounds that form one large wound. The wound extends completely through skin and subcutis and into the abdominal cavity. Colon and omentum has herniated from the wound. Found within the depths of this wound beneath the omentum is a Nokia brand cell phone further described below.

On the left epigastrium and superior to the large complex wound is a cluster of six stab wounds (labeled #14, #16, #17, #18, #19 and #21) all composed of blunt ends opposed by pointed ends. The wounds are situated within an 8 x 7 cm area and vary from 1.8 to 3 cm. Most are oriented obliquely from upper left to lower left to lower right with lower blunt ends opposed by pointed ends, but the two most lateral wounds are horizontal with blunt lateral ends. The most superior of these wounds extends through the skin and subcutis but not into the abdominal cavity. All of the other wounds extend completely through the skin and subcutis of the abdominal wall and into the peritoneal cavity where there are injuries described below under "Internal Examination."

On the mid-upper abdomen near the large complex wound is a tripolar 10 x 5 stab-incised wound (labeled #20). The horizontal component is a stab wound that extends into the abdominal cavity. The vertical component is a superficial incised wound extending just into subcutis. The wound focally reaches he large gaping wound.

On the lateral right upper abdomen is a cluster of six stab wounds (#22, #23, #24, #25 and #26). Most are oriented vertically with inferior blunt ends opposed by pointed ends. The stab wounds occupy an area 18 x 14 cm and vary from 2.2 to 3 cm long. All perforate the skin and subcutis of the right lateral and mid abdomen extending into the peritoneal cavity. Along the lower border of this cluster of stab wounds is a horizontal long linear abrasion. A vertical-oriented stab wound (labeled #27) is at the medial outskirts of this group and is partially incorporated into the large complex wound, effectively becoming part of that wound.

On the mid-lower abdomen is a 13 cm long horizontal superficial incised wound (labeled #38) that does not extend through the skin, but is intersected by another oblique 5.5 cm long superficial incised wound. Also on the mid-lower abdomen near the lower border of the large complex wound are four horizontally-oriented slit-like stab wounds (labeled #40, #41, #42, and #43) that are all 3 cm long. Most have a left lateral blunt ends opposed by pointed ends All of these stab wounds extend through the anterior abdominal wall into the peritoneal cavity causing injuries described below under "Internal Examination." On the mid-lower abdomen is a horizontal gaping 19 cm long incised wound that gapes into 1.6 cm (labeled #39). This long incised wound extends completely through the abdominal wall into the peritoneal cavity. Just below that is another horizontal stab-incised wound (labeled #44), 3 cm long, which also extends through the abdominal wall into the peritoneal cavity causing injuries described below under "Internal Examination." These wounds on the mid-lower abdomen occupy a 12 x 9 cm area.

On the right lateral abdomen is a cluster of six haphazardly-oriented stab wounds, all with blunt ends opposed by pointed ends (#28, #29 #30, #31, #32, and #33). These are within the 18 x 14 cm zone described above under the cluster of wounds in the lateral right upper abdomen and are within the range of 2.2 to 3 cm in length. All of these wounds also extend completely through the abdominal wall into the peritoneal cavity resulting in injuries described below under "Internal Examination."

On the left lateral abdomen is a horizontal 2.2. cm stab wound (labeled #37) composed of a left lateral blunt end opposed by a pointed end that also extends completely through the abdominal wall into the peritoneal cavity.

On the left lateral pectoral area is a horizontal 1.8 cm long stab wound (labeled #46) composed of a lateral blunt end opposed by a pointed end. This wound perforates the skin and subcutis and perforates the left chest wall through the fourth intercostal space, laterally, and penetrates into the left upper lung lobe for a depth of 6 cm. The wound path is oriented from left to right and horizontal for a depth of 6 cm. On the left breast is a horizontal 3.2 cm long stab wound (labeled #45) composed of a left lateral blunt end opposed by a pointed end. This wound penetrates into left breast for a depth of 8 cm oriented front to back, left to right, and slightly downward. Posterior to that on the left lateral chest wall is a horizontal 3.5 cm long stab wound that gapes to 1.8 cm (labeled #47) composed of a posterior blunt end opposed by a pointed end. This wound perforates the skin and the subcutis of the left chest and penetrates into the left chest cavity coursing left to right and slightly downward, at least 11 cm deep. On the lower left chest is a horizontal 1.2 cm long, superficial stab wound (labeled #48) that extends just into the subcutis of the lower lateral left breast, oriented left to right and slightly upward. On the left costal margin is a horizontal 3.5 cm long stab wound (labeled #36) that is beveled inferiorly. This wound perforates the skin and penetrates into soft tissues but does not penetrate into the abdomen, oriented left to right and slightly upward for a depth of 10.5 cm. Lateral to that wound and situated on the lower lateral left chest wall is an obliquely-oriented 2.5 cm long stab wound (labeled #49) composed of an upper posterior blunt end opposed by a pointed end. This wound perforates skin but stays within soft tissues coursing back to front, slightly left to right, and upward for a depth of 5 cm. Below this wound is a horizontal 2.6 cm long stab wound (labeled #50) also composed of a posterior blunt end opposed by a pointed end. This wound perforates the skin and subcutis of the left flank and penetrates through the left tenth intercostal space, posteriorly, and enters the chest cavity for a depth of 10 cm. Situated 0.2 cm below and parallel to the wound #50 is a 2.5 cm long stab wound (labeled #75). This wound also perforates the skin and subcutis and follows the same wound path as #50 penetrating into the left chest cavity through the tenth intercostal space, possibly also into the posterior LUQ of the abdomen.

There are multiple perforating stab wounds of the left arm. On the posterolateral left upper arm is a vertical 3.5 cm long stab wound (labeled #53) composed of an inferior blunt end opposed by a pointed end that perforates the skin and subcutis and penetrates 6 cm deep, oriented lateral to medial and slightly back to front. Below that is a jagged 4.5 cm stab-incised wound (labeled #54) that also perforates skin and penetrates into soft tissues of the upper arm. Also on the posterior upper arm is a pair of side-by-side stab wounds (labeled #55 and #56), 4.2 and 4 cm long, that are parallel and represent entrance/exit defects of the same wound path only 1.5 cm apart. On the lateral upper arm is a vertical 3 cm stab wound (labeled #52) composed of a superior blunt end opposed by a pointed end. This perforates the skin and subcutis, and courses lateral to medial into soft tissue. Side by side jagged stab-incised wounds (labeled #57 and #58) 6.2 cm and 4 cm long, are on the lateral left upper arm near the elbow. These both course lateral to medial and slightly upward, and then both exit the medial surface through a pair of side-by-side 3 cm exit defects (labeled #61 and #62) for a maximum wound length of 11 cm. Also on the lateral upper arm is a longitudinal 5.5 cm long stab-incised wound composed of a superior blunt end opposed by a pointed end (labeled #59). This wound path courses within subcutis for a distance of 2 cm and then exits the posteromedial arm near the elbow through a chevron-shaped 3 cm long defect (labeled #60). On the left ulnar border of the forearm near the elbow is an oblique 3.5 long superficial incised wound that does not extend completely through the skin (labeled #66). On the proximal forearm near the elbow is a complex tripolar 5 x 5 cm stab-incised wound (labeled #64) that leads to several separate wound paths. One path courses medially for 2 cm then exits the medial elbow through a 3.5 cm defect (labeled #67); another path courses anteriorly and lateral to the medial for 9 cm. incises the proximal radium, and then exits the medial antecubital fossa through a jagged 1.8 cm defect (labeled #68); and another path courses proximally for a short distance and then exits through a small horizontal defect (labeled #65) on the elbow.

Extending longitudinally along the medial right thigh is a vertically-oriented incised wound (labeled #69). This wound measures 27 cm long and gapes to approximately 3 cm. The wound extends through the skin and into deep subcutaneous soft tissues. At the proximal end the wound becomes a stab wound that courses upward and medial to lateral for a depth of 11 cm, passing medial to the femoral artery and vein without gross injury. There is no significant hemorrhage within this incised wound or along the stab wound path.

Over the left hip is a curvilinear 7 cm long stab-incised wound (labeled #51) that gapes to 2 cm, composed of two pointed ends. This courses lateral to medial and penetrates into the abdominal cavity. On the anterior left thigh is a pair of stab wounds. The superior wound is a 1.1 cm stab (labeled #70) that penetrates 5.5 cm deep, oriented front to back and slightly lateral to medial, staying within the soft tissue. Inferior to that is an oblique 2.4 cm long stab wound (labeled #71) composed of a superior blunt end opposed by a pointed end. The wound path courses lateral to medial and slightly downward through skeletal muscle anterior to the femur for a depth of 11.5 cm. There is fresh hemorrhage along this wound path.

On the left upper back are three horizontal stab wounds. The most superior is a 3 cm long stab wound (labeled #72) composed of a lateral blunt end opposed by a medial end. This wound path perforates the skin and soft tissues of the upper mid-back coursing back to front and slightly upward but staying within soft tissue for a depth of 11.5 cm. The middle wound is over the lateral left scapula area and consists of a horizontal 3 cm long stab wound (labeled #73) composed of a medial blunt end opposed by a pointed end. This perforates the skin and soft tissues coursing left to right, slightly back to front and slightly downward until it impacts the back of the spine for a depth of 11 cm. The lower of the three wounds is a 2.5 cm long stab wound (labeled #74) composed of a lateral blunt end opposed by a pointed end. This also courses left to right, slightly back to front and slightly downward within soft tissue for a depth of 9.5 cm.

Northup, Jr. Oliver. Postmortem Date: 04-15-2013. Time: 16:00. Place of death: Usual residence. Date found: 04-14-2013. Time: 22:01. Age: 87. Sex: Male. Height: 71 in. Weight: 191 lb.

Autopsy Findings

1. Incised wounds (3) of forehead, perimortem

2. Stab-incised wound (1) of left parietal scalp into left temporalis muscle, perimortem
   A. Depth 7 cm (2 ¾ in.)

3. Superficial stab and incised wounds (5) of face

4. Stab wounds (2) of both cheeks, perimortem

5. Stab wound (1) of right neck.
   A. Perforation of right jugular vein

6. Stab wounds (3) of left neck.
   A. perforation of left jugular vein.
   B. maximum depth: 5.5 cm (2 in.)

7. Stab wounds (2) on right pectoral area.
   A. both penetrate into right chest cavity, incising right ribs 5 and 6.

8. Stab wound (1) into left lateral chest incising left eighth rib.
   A. penetration into soft tissue
   B. depth: 11 cm. (4 ½ in.)

9. Stab wound (1) into left lateral chest incising left eighth rib
   A. incision of left lung.

10. Multiple stab wounds (33) of abdomen.
    A. All penetrate through anterior abdominal wall into peritoneal cavity
    B. Perforations of stomach, small bowel and colon
    C. Perforations of liver
    E. Incisions of spleen
    E. Perforation of abdominal aorta
    F. Bilateral hemothoraces and scant hemoperitumeum.

11. Large, gaping complex stab-incised wound (1) of left upper abdomen.
   A. Herniation of small bowel and mesentery.
   B. Foreign object (drinking glass) found within depth of wound.

12. Defense-type incised wounds (3) of right hand and forearm.
   A. Incision of proximal phalanx of right index finger.
13. Stab wounds (5) of lower leg.
   A. Three wounds perforate the lower leg and ankle.
   B. Possibly represent "defense" wounds.

Causes of death: multiple stab wounds

Opinion: 61 separate wounds are enumerated.

Mark Super, M.D. 6-23-2013. Investigator: Deputy Coroner G. Moya Witnesses: Investigators T. Souza and R. Strange, Yolo County District Attorney's office; Sergeant M. Munoz and CSI Officer M. Alfaro, Davis Police Department; Deputy Coroner G. Moya and Intern J. Foster, Yolo County Sheriff-Coroner's Office.

Evidence of Injury

On the forehead are three incised wounds. These consist of an obliquely-oriented 7 cm long incised wound (labeled #1) oriented from upper left to lower right; and oblique 5.56 cm long incised wound (labeled #3) on the lower mid-forehead oriented from upper right to lower left that extends just into the left eyebrow; and a horizontal 5.56 cm long incised wound (labeled #2) of the left mid-forehead. All three incised wounds extend completely through the skin to the surface of the skull. The underlying skill surface is not marked and the incised wounds are free of significant surrounding hemorrhage.

On the left parietal scalp is a horizontal 4.5 cm long stab/incised wound (labeled #4). The superior edge is thinly abraded. The wound extends completely through the scalp almost to the surface of the skull but leads to a stab wound track, 7 cm deep, which extends straight downward and slightly front to back into the left temporalis muscle.

On the side of the nose is a pair of oblique superficial incised wounds, each 1.5 cm long, oriented form upper posterior to lower anterior (labeled #5 and #6). The more inferior wound is #6 and has a pointed end opposed by a blunt end. These wounds extend just through the skin and are free of significant hemorrhage.

Situated just above the left angle of the mouth is a 1.4 cm long horizontal stab wound (labeled #10) that is composed of an anterior blunt end opposed by a pointed end. This wound extends through the skin and subcutis angling downward and left to right for a depth of 3 cm into soft tissue without penetrating into the mouth.

Below the right lateral canthal area of the right eye is a vertical 1.8 cm long superficial incised wound (labeled #15) composed of two pointed ends. This extends just through skin and is without soft tissue hemorrhage. Extending horizontally along the lower left eyelid is a 4 cm long superficial incised wound (labeled #8) that extends just through skin and is free of subcutaneous soft tissue hemorrhage. Situated over the left inferior orbital rim is a 1 cm long superficial stab-incised wound (labeled #7) that barely gets through skin and is free of subcutaneous soft tissue hemorrhage.

On the lower right cheek is an oblique 1.5 cm stab wound (labeled #9) composed of a posterior/inferior blunt end opposed by a pointed end. The wound path extends through skin and into deep soft tissue surrounded by ecchymosis. Liquid blood oozes from this wound. The wound perforates skeletal muscle and incises the right jugular vein associated with surrounding soft tissue hemorrhage.

On the left lateral upper neck is a group of three stab-incised wounds. The most superior of this group is a horizontal 3 cm long stab wound (labeled #11) composed of an anterior blunt end opposed by a pointed end. Extending upward and forward from the posterior end is a 4 cm long linear abrasion suggestive of a knife tip drag. The wound path perforates skin and soft tissues of the left lateral upper neck extending 5.5 cm deep and oriented front to back, slightly left to right and slightly downward. Fresh hemorrhage is in this wound track. The middle wound is a horizontal 3.5 cm long stab-incised wound (labeled #12) composed of and anterior blunt end opposed by a pointed end. This also extends through skin and into deep soft tissue oriented left to right, slightly front to back and very slightly upward for a depth of 5.5 cm. Liquid blood oozes from this wound and the wound track is hemorrhagic. The most inferior of the three stab wounds is a 2.7 cm long stab wound (labeled #13) composed of an anterior blunt end opposed by a pointed end. This wound also extends through the skin and into deep soft tissue oriented similar to wound #12, also for a depth of 5.5 cm. The three stab wounds on the left side of the neck have a relatively common path extending deep into the left side of the neck. Along those paths is a perforation of the left jugular vein surrounded by hemorrhage.

On the left upper abdomen is an obliquely oriented, large gaping stab-incised wound (labeled #50), 23 cm long that gapes to 9 cm, oriented from upper right to lower left. This wound has jagged edges which may be due to the wound being an incorporation of several stab wounds. The wound extends completely through skin subcutis and the anterior abdominal wall. A large portion of small bowel and omentum has herniated from this wound. Also, a small drinking glass has been placed into this wound, as described below. The glass is not broken and is stained only by body fluids, as best as I can tell.

On the right pectoral area is a pair of horizontal stab wounds (labeled #16 and #17). Both wounds are composed of medial blunt ends opposed by pointed ends. The wounds measure 3.3 and 3.7 cm long, respectively. Both wounds extend through skin and subcutaneous soft tissue extending into the right chest cavity oriented front to back, slightly right to left and slightly upward. Stab wound #16 incises the right sixth rib and stab wound #17 incises the fifth rib. The perforations of the right chest wall are associated with fresh hemorrhage.

On the upper lateral left chest near the apex of the axilia is a vertical stab wound (labeled #52). The wound is 2.7 cm long and composed of an inferior blunt and opposed by a pointed end. The stab wound extends through skin and subcutis into soft tissues of the left pectoral area angling left to right, front to back and slightly upward towards the left clavicle for a depth of 11 cm.

On the left lateral chest wall is a horizontal 3.2 cm long stab wound (labeled #54) composed of a posterior blunt end opposed by a pointed end. The wound path perforates the left chest wall through the eighth intercostal space, incising the left eighth rib, and penetrating into the left chest cavity.

Situated on the mid-upper abdomen above the large gaping stab-incised wound is a group of nine horizontally oriented stab wounds (labeled #18, #19, #21, #22, #23, #24, #25, #26, and #27) that vary in length from 1.7 to 3.2 cm. They occupy an area 10 x 9 cm that extends from the skin over the lower sternum to the mid-epigastrium and left upper abdomen. Some are composed of right lateral blunt ends opposed by pointed ends but some have left lateral blunt ends. The most superior of these wounds (#18) perforates skin and impacts the sternum where it stops. All of the other stab wounds in this group extend completely through the anterior abdominal wall penetrating into the peritoneal cavity resulting in injuries described below under "Internal Examination."

On the right abdomen is a group of ten stab wounds 20 x 15 cm in area (#20, #28, #29, #30, #31, #35, #36, #37, and #38). The wounds vary from 1.2 cm to 3 cm long and most are horizontal, but some are obliquely oriented from upper left to lower right. All have blunt ends opposed by pointed ends with blunt ends predominately on the left. All but one of these wounds perforate the skin and subcutis of the right abdomen and penetrate into the peritoneal cavity resulting in injuries described below under "Internal Examination." The most inferior of these wounds (#36) is a superficial stab-incised wound that extends only into subcutis.

On the mid-upper abdomen along the lower border of the large gaping stab-incised wound is a group of four stab wounds (#33, #34, #39 and #40). The largest of these (#34) is a 6 x 7.2 cm tripolar complex wound that may represent more than one stab wound. The wounds occupy an 8 x 6 cm area situated superior to the umbilicus but inferior to the large gaping stab-incised wound and vary in length from 1.8 to 2.7 cm long. All are wounds composed of blunt ends opposed by pointed ends and most are obliquely oriented from upper left to lower right. All perforate the skin and subcutaneous soft tissues of the mid-abdomen and penetrate into the peritoneal cavity resulting injuries described below under "Internal Examination."

On the left lower abdomen and near the umbilicus is a group of four stab wounds (#41, #44, #45, and #46). All but one perforate the skin and subcutis of the left lateral abdominal wall and penetrate into the peritoneal cavity. #49 extends only into the subcutis. #51 is situated along the lower edge of the large, gaping, stab-incised wound.

These stab wounds occupy an area 9 x 8 cm and vary from 2.4 to 4 cm long. All are wounds composed of blunt ends opposed by pointed ends and most are obliquely oriented from upper left to lower right. All four stab wounds extend completely through skin and subcutis and lower left abdominal wall penetrating into the peritoneal cavity.

Also on the left lower abdomen and is a pair of obliquely oriented stab wounds (labeled # 42 and #43). Each is 3 cm long and composed of an upper left blunt end opposed by a pointed end. Both perforate the skin and subcutis of the lower left abdomen and penetrate into the peritoneal cavity.

On the left lateral abdomen is a group of four stab wounds (#47, #48, #49 and #51 that measure up to 2 cm long. All but one perforate the skin of the lower left abdominal wall and penetrate into the peritoneal cavity. #49 extends only into subcutis. #51 is situated along the lower edge of the large, gaping stab-incised wound.

On the web space between the right index and middle fingers is a 3.5 cm long incised stab wound (labeled #55) that incises skin and subcutis of the hand and incises the medial base of the proximal phalanx and severs a tendon. All associated with fresh hemorrhage. On the palmar right thumb is a 0.8 superficial cut (labeled #57) that extends through skin and into subcutis. These wounds of the right hand and forearm are considered "defensive-type" injuries.

On the lateral lower leg is a vertical 3.7 cm long stab wound (labeled #58) composed of a superior blunt end opposed by a pointed end. The wound path perforates through skin and subcutis of the left lower leg and perforates the entire lower leg exiting on the medial aspect through 2.4 cm long defect (labeled #59) composed of a superior blunt end opposed by a pointed end. Near the left lateral malleolus is an oblique 3.1 cm stab wound (labeled #64) composed of a posterior/superior blunt end oppose by a pointed end. This wound path perforates skin and subcutaneous soft tissue of the left ankle passing through the left lower leg at boot top level exiting on the medial aspect above the left lower leg at boot top level exiting on the medial aspect above the ankle joint through a 2 cm defect (labeled #63) also compose of a superior blunt end opposed by a pointed end. On the anteromedial left ankle is a perforating stab wound that is composed of entrance and exit defects (labeled #61 and #62) that are each vertically oriented wounds that vary from 3.8 to 3.4 cm long oriented vertically with inferior blunt ends opposed by pointed ends separated by a subcutaneous wound track. I am unable to tell which is the entrance and which is the exit wound.

On the anterolateral left lower leg is an oblique 2 cm long stab wound (labeled #60) composed of a superior blunt end opposed by a pointed end. This wound penetrates into soft tissues of the lower leg. On top of the left foot near the base of the little toe is a 1.2 long superficial stab wound (labeled #65 that extends just through skin and into underlying soft tissue. On the anteromedial left lower leg is a horizontal 1.7 cm long linear abrasion. On the back of the left hand between the knuckles of the index and middle finger is a 0.5 cm red-purple contusion.

Acknowledgements

A murderer's own account of his crime is a primary source that readers should be able to appraise for themselves, but therein lies a story. I witnessed Daniel Marsh's entire interview in Yolo Superior Court, which allows no recording or use of a computer. Nobody can write in longhand as fast as people talk, particularly someone recovering from a broken hand, as I was at the time. I also discovered that the regular trial transcript does not include video materials shown in the courtroom. The sound was rather unclear, so the court provided each jury member with a full transcript of the marathon interview. That was not available to writers during the trial, but Chief Assistant Deputy District Attorney Michael Cabral told me to check in "when this is over." I did, and thanks to Deputy District Attorney Amanda Zambor and the Yolo County District Attorney's Office for providing the document.

The author thanks the Yolo County Sheriff's Department for releasing the autopsy reports, which had remained sealed during the trial. These documents enable the two murder victims to tell a key part of their story.

The author again thanks relatives and friends of the victims for helping me get to know them. Thanks to Claudia's daughter Victoria Hurd for the circular emblem labeled "Live like Claudia & Chip." As I wrote in the *Davis Enterprise* on December 16, 2014, "These were loving people, peaceful people, spiritual people. Chip and Claudia did not deserve to go out this way, and neither does anybody else."

Readers of *Killer Confession* might also like:

Lloyd Billingsley covered the Daniel Marsh trial start to finish. In this book, readers share the view from a front-row seat.

Selections from the reviews:

"A thought-provoking, fast-paced page turner, which fans of crime stories are sure to enjoy."

"Mr. Billingsley's meticulous historical research and accessible writing style makes for compulsive reading. It's the perfect book for fans of history and crime stories. One note of caution: don't start reading unless you have lots of time because you won't be able to stop until the last page."

"The story of this well-publicized murder is both riveting and disturbing, to be sure. But Billingsley also documents the legal decisions and details, in a way any motivated reader can appreciate."

Readers might also like:

What readers say:

"A shapely read out of a massive mountain of data...dovetailing stories. . . a lot of sleuthing...a job you can be proud of."

–Freida Batten, first wife of murder victim Jim Batten.

"Her trial seemed like a real 'pity party' and less justice. Good job, Lloyd Billingsley, for bringing this out in your book."

–Diane Neal-Barrett, niece of murder victim Jim Batten.

"This is the third book I've read by Lloyd Billingsley. As with the others, he gives an extremely precise attention to details, exhibiting the true journalist that he is. Hard to put the book down."

–Mat Marucci, Sacramento jazz artist.

"A quick, exciting read if you're into true crime stories. Billingsley is a good writer and a terrific reporter...an author who's not afraid to overturn rocks, political and social, and reveal the slime underneath."

–Harry Cheney, Chapman University professor and film editor

"Mr. Billingsley's book," wrote Charlton Heston, "is the best exploration I've seen of the Hollywood blacklist and the Communist Party's role in that conflict."

"Mr. Billingsley's book tells the story of the battle for the soul of Hollywood," wrote Herb Romerstein, co-author of *Stalin's Secret Agents*.

Also by Lloyd Billingsley:

"A virtuoso performance," writes Peter Collier. "A unique trip log of a writer who has been singularly engaged with the issues of his day."

www.ingramcontent.com/pod-product-compliance
Lightning Source LLC
Chambersburg PA
CBHW031643040426
42453CB00006B/197